CROCHET

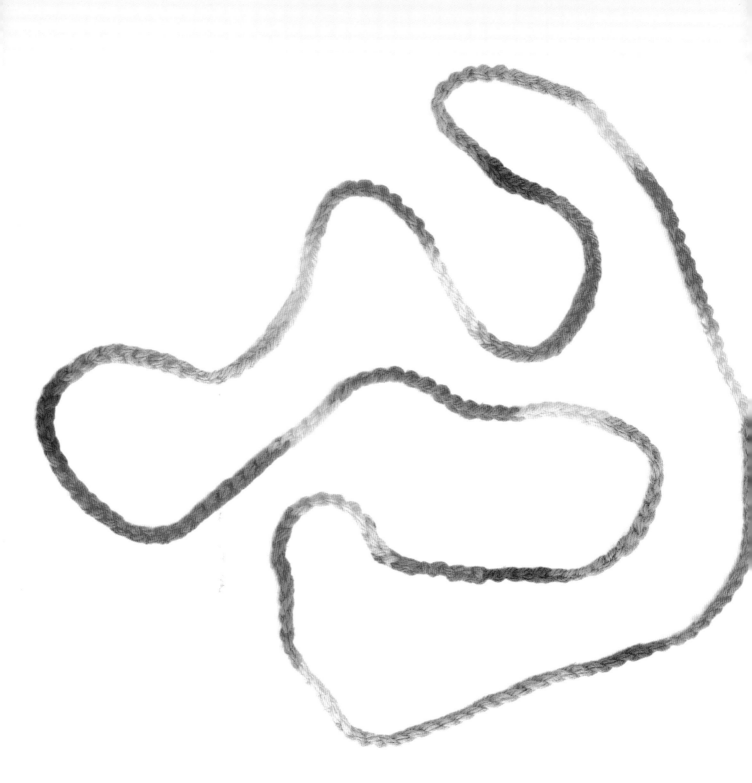

Crochet

Fantastic Jewelry, Hats, Purses, Pillows & More

Jane Davis

LARK BOOKS

A Division of Sterling Publishing Co., Inc.
New York

EDITOR:

JANE LaFERLA

ART DIRECTOR:

DANA IRWIN

PHOTOGRAPHER:

SANDRA STAMBAUGH

COVER DESIGNER:

BARBARA ZARETSKY

ILLUSTRATOR:

AUGUST HOERR

ASSISTANT EDITOR:

REBECCA GUTHRIE

ASSISTANT ART DIRECTOR:

LANCE WILLE

EDITORIAL ASSISTANCE:

DELORES GOSNELL

The Library of Congress has cataloged the hardcover edition as follows:

Davis, Jane, 1959-
  Crochet : fantastic jewelry, hats, purses, pillows & more / by Jane Davis.
      p. cm. — (Kids' crafts)
  Includes index.
  ISBN 1-57990-477-7 (hardcover)
  1. Crocheting—Patterns. I. Title. II. Series.
TT825.D3824 2005
746.43'4041—dc22

2004013288

10 9 8 7 6 5 4 3 2 1

Published by Lark Books, A Division of
Sterling Publishing Co., Inc.
387 Park Avenue South, New York, N.Y. 10016

First Paperback Edition 2007
© 2005, Jane Davis

Distributed in Canada by Sterling Publishing,
c/o Canadian Manda Group, 165 Dufferin Street
Toronto, Ontario, Canada M6K 3H6

Distributed in the United Kingdom by GMC Distribution Services,
Castle Place, 166 High Street, Lewes, East Sussex, England BN7 1XU

Distributed in Australia by Capricorn Link (Australia) Pty Ltd.,
P.O. Box 704, Windsor, NSW 2756 Australia

If you have questions or comments about this book, please contact:
Lark Books
67 Broadway
Asheville, NC 28801
(828) 253-0467

Manufactured in China

ISBN 13: 978-1-57990-477-7 (hardcover)
ISBN 10: 1-57990-477-7 (hardcover)
ISBN 13: 978-1-60059-138-9 (paperback)
ISBN 10: 1-60059-138-8 (paperback)

For information about custom editions, special sales, premium and corporate purchases, please contact Sterling Special Sales Department at 800-805-5489 or specialsales@sterlingpub.com.

Table of Contents

Introduction

rochet has been around for a very long time. The word "crochet" comes from the French word for hook. But more than 100 years ago, when hooks were commonly made from fish bones or old silver spoons, crochet was

sometimes called "shepherd's knitting," because shepherds often did their crochet work as they watched their flocks of sheep out in the fields. Mittens were one of the most common items made from the basic crochet slip stitch. They were prized for their thickness because they kept hands warm and dry in the cold wet winters of Scotland, Norway, and Sweden. But wherever winters were cold, men, women, and children alike worked stitches to make warm clothing.

WHAT IS CROCHET?

Today, all kinds of people who like to make things with their hands enjoy crocheting. It's basically just pulling yarn through loops with a hook, so it's easy to learn. And because you crochet using yarn and a few inexpensive tools and supplies, you can be on your way to creating something in no time! Before you know it you can make a hat to wear, a scarf to keep you warm, balls to play with, pillows for your room, or a perfectly pleasing pink pig to keep you company.

IS IT EASY?

Yes! This book will give you all the basic information you'll need for completing the projects in this book—start to finish! You'll learn the words and phrases you need to know, and all about tools and materials. You'll find illustrations that will show you how to make the stitches. After that, there's a section that takes you beyond the basics if you want to learn more. It has more information about advanced stitches and using different yarns.

WHAT CAN I MAKE?

There are 30 terrific projects to choose from. You can make game pieces, balls, bags, jewelry, cool stuff for your room, and things to wear. The first section has beginning projects to get you started. The next three sections are organized by the type of crochet you'll make, like squares, circles, or netting. The last two sections have projects that take more time to make, or use beads, thinner cord, and smaller hooks—you'll want to be comfortable with crocheting before challenging yourself with those projects.

Getting Started

WORDS AND PHRASES

There are many words and phrases used in crochet that have special meanings that might be new to you. The following section will help you learn about them.

ABBREVIATIONS

Abbreviations are the secret code of crochet. They're used in instructions to save space, otherwise instructions would take up pages and pages if the whole words were used. Since using abbreviations is an important part of knowing how to crochet, this book makes it easy for you to learn.

In this chapter and in the first two project sections, the instructions are all written out with the abbreviations in parentheses so you can become familiar with them. As you continue making the projects, you'll notice that some of the last projects in a section are written in all abbreviations. When you come to these projects, you'll already be familiar with the abbreviations and will sail right throught the instructions.

Abbreviations are usually easy to figure out. For example, stitch is st, chain becomes ch, single crochet sc, and double crochet dc. When instructions are written out with abbreviations in parentheses it might look like this: Yarn over (yo), and pull the yarn through both loops (lps) on the hook (hk). Or like this: Round 4: Single crochet in the next 2 stitches, and then make 2 single crochet in the next stitch 6 times or repeat across, when you're done you will have 24 stitches. ([sc in next 2 sts, 2 sc in next st] 6 times (24 sts total).) This may look confusing to you now, but before you know it, you won't have to think twice about the abbreviations—and you'll be able to decode any project you attempt.

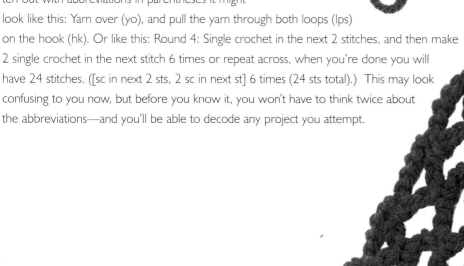

Below is a list of the abbreviations used in this book. You might want to copy this page and keep it with you when you're working on the projects.

bc	bead crochet
beg	begin/beginning
ch	chain
ch-1,	one chain,
ch-2, ...	two chains, ...
chs	chains
ch sp	chain space
dc	double crochet
dec	decrease
hdc	half double crochet
hk	hook
inc	increase
lp	loop
pm	place marker
rep	repeat
reps	repeats
rnd	round
sc	single crochet
sk	skip
sl st	slip stitch
st	stitch
sts	stitches
tog	together
yo	yarn over

BLOCKING

Blocking helps you get your finished crochet in shape. A lot of times when you crochet something, especially when you're working around and around in a spiral, the finished item ends up slanting in one direction, or is not exactly the right size. To block, you wet the piece, pull it into the finished shape you want it to be, and let it dry. You can wet the crochet by soaking it in water, or have an adult help you use the steam from a steam iron. If you soak it in water, you need to roll it tightly in a towel to get most of the water out before you block it, so it will dry in a reasonable amount of time, usually overnight.

BRACKETS [ ] OR PARENTHESES ( )

These are used to enclose a group of instructions that you will repeat. After the brackets or parentheses, the instructions will tell you how many

9

times to repeat the instructions. It will look like this: [sc in next 2 sts, 2 sc in next st] 6 times. This means that you single crochet in the next 2 stitches, and then make 2 single crochet in the next stitch and that you do this 6 times. Parentheses are also used at the beginning of instructions and after an increase or decrease to tell you how many stitches there are in the row or round. It will look like this: (24 sts total). And of course, they're also used to show abbreviations described on page 8.

CLUSTERS

Clusters are used as decorative designs in a pattern. They make a line of crochet that curls. That's why the tail of the Roly Poly Pig on page 66 is made this way. A cluster is made from several partial stitches. Instead of completing a stitch by making the last yarn over and pulling it through the loop, you make the last yarn over, keep it on the hook, and then repeat the steps for the stitch in one or more stitches. You'll end up with loops on the hook from each yarn over plus the loop on the hook. You finally finish the cluster by pulling all the loops from the yarn overs through the loop on the hook. This is also used for decreasing, since you reduce all those stitches down to one stitch for the next row.

DECREASE (DEC)

Sometimes you have to get rid of stitches in order to shape a piece. That's when you need to decrease so there will be fewer stitches in the next row or round. There are two basic ways to decrease in crochet. The easiest way is to just skip one or more stitches so you'll have fewer stitches to work with in the next row or round. The other way is to change the type of stitch or the pattern you're using to one that gives you fewer stitches in the following rows.

FOUNDATION

This is the beginning of your project that starts with the slipknot and chain (see page 15).

GAUGE

The gauge is how many stitches there are in a row and a column measured from a 4-inch square of crochet. Patterns will give you a gauge. You want your crocheting to match that measurement so your project will end up with the same finished size the pattern gives. Having the right gauge is very important when making something like clothing, because you want it to be the right size. It's not as important when making something like the ball on page 52 that can be any size.

It's a good idea to make up a sample piece of crochet that's 4 inches square before beginning a project. Then you can compare your number of stitches to the pattern's gauge. If your stitches are small and there are too many of them, you may be holding the yarn too tightly as you crochet. If the stitches are big and there are not enough, you may be holding the yarn too loosely. You can adjust your gauge by holding the yarn differently or by using a larger or smaller hook than the size listed in the instructions.

OOOPs!!!

One of the most common things that happens when you're learning to crochet is that your rectangle or square ends up looking more like a triangle or will be wider at one end than the other. This happens when you accidentally increase or decrease in one or more rows as you work. That's why it's always good to check that you've made the correct number of stitches after you complete every few rows.

INCREASE (INC)

Sometimes you have to add stitches in order to shape a piece. That's when you need to increase so there will be more stitches in the next row or round. There are three basic ways to increase in crochet. One way is to work two or more stitches in the same stitch. Another way is to work one more stitch at the end or beginning of the row. The other way is like decreasing, where you change the type of stitch or pattern to one that will give you more stitches in the following rows.

PICOT

A picot is a little decorative bump that's usually made in the middle of a crochet chain. To make a picot,

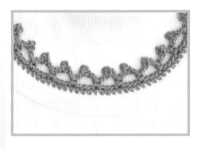

you make the number of chains the pattern tells you to, and then you make a slip stitch in the chain that is several stitches away from the hook (the instructions will say how many). When you continue to do this, you'll get a wavy line of crochet that works well for edging.

ROUND

This is one row of stitches when you are working around in a spiral, like when you make a ball. This is the perfect place for using your stitch markers. By placing a stitch marker in the first or last stitch of the round, it's

easy to know where you begin each round.

ROW

This is one row of stitches across a piece. To make it easier to understand how to begin the next row, it's almost better to think of a row

11

as one "level." To get to the next level, you need to chain one or more stitches at the end of the row. These extra chains will help you get your work up to the next level. In fact, these chain stitches are sometimes called "step-ups."

SHELL

Shells are made by working two or more crochet stitches in the same place to create a shell or fan shape. Shells can be large like the second row on the ruffled hair scrunchie on page 34, or they can be small like the increases for Saturn's rings in the Space Balls project on page 60.

TAIL OR END

This is a loose end of yarn. Tails are made at the beginning or end of a project, or if you change yarns during crocheting. To make your work neat, you weave the tails in using a tapestry needle

TENSION

This is how tight or loose you work your stitches. Loose tension makes your crochet work more soft and drapey, while a tight tension creates a stiff fabric. You need to use a tighter tension for projects like the balls so they will hold their stuffing, while using a loose tension is good for clothing because it makes the fabric comfortable to wear. The tension you use, along with the size of the hook and thickness of the yarn determines the gauge of your project.

TURN

When you get to the end of a row you need to turn your crochet work around to the other side. When you do this, you can work the next row back across the stitches you just made. You're always working from right to left across the top of your crocheting. When you work in a spiral, you just keep going around and around—the beginning instructions for working a spiral say, "do not turn."

WEAVE IN THE ENDS

Weaving in the ends lets you hide any yarn tails in the crochet. To weave in an end, you first thread a tapestry needle with the tail. Then you weave the yarn in for about an inch or two. If you cut the remaining tail close to the crocheting after weaving, it won't show.

WORK EVEN

This means to continue working the pattern without any increases or decreases.

WORKING THROUGH TWO THICKNESSES

You can attach two or more pieces of crochet together by making a stitch through all the pieces. To do this, you insert the hook into the edge of one piece that's on top and the edge of another piece underneath, then you make a stitch that will hold both pieces together. An example of this technique is used for the Pencil Case on page 42 when you need to attach the sides.

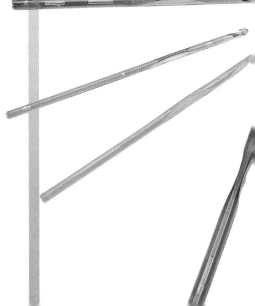

Keep It Neat

As you begin to make projects, you'll want them to look as well made as possible—and that means paying attention to details. The neater you make your work, the better it will look. Try and make all your stitches the same size, and carefully hide any loose yarn ends in your work so they don't show.

Tools and Materials

O ne of the best parts of crochet is that you won't go broke buying tools and yarn to make your projects. You can find what you need just about anywhere you buy craft materials.

HOOKS

A hook is *the* tool in crochet. Hooks come in many sizes, from tiny steel hooks where you can hardly see the hook at the end— they're the most delicate and are used for making lace and jewelry— to thick plastic hooks, thicker than a wooden spoon handle, for making blankets and rugs. The hooks are sized by their width just below the hook section. The size can be in numbers, showing how thick the hook is in millimeters, or in letters. What's really confusing is that they can differ from maker to maker. It's always best to look at the millimeter size if you want to make sure you have the correct size hook. Look at the chart of crochet hook sizes on page 21 to see all the different sizes there are.

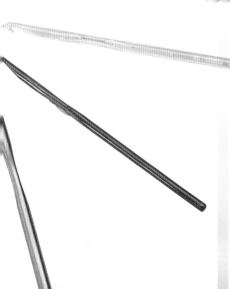

STITCH MARKERS

Stitch markers help you easily find your place when you need to. They are small plastic or metal loops or spirals that you slide into your crocheting to mark a stitch or a side seam. You use stitch markers to help mark the beginning of a round so you know when to make increases in the same place—like when you're making a ball. When the instructions say place marker (pm) that means to slide the stitch marker into the top two loops of the stitch you just made. As you crochet a round, you always move the marker to the last stitch of the old round, or the first stitch of the new round

TAPESTRY NEEDLES

Tapestry needles help you weave in yarn ends to hide them in the crocheting. They are large, round-ended needles with eyes that are big enough for threading your yarn. They come in a range of sizes and are numbered

from the smallest, size 28, to the largest, size 13. The larger sizes work best with most yarns. The easiest way to thread the needle is to first fold the yarn over the needle, pinch the fold tightly, slide the fold off the needle, and then push it through the eye of the needle.

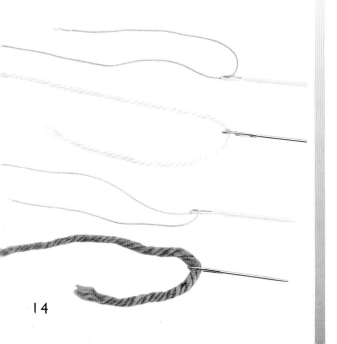

YARN

Yarn comes in many sizes (thin to thick), textures (smooth to nubbly), and colors (more than you can imagine!). Yarn sizes are called "weights," and some of the most common weights you'll use are fine, light, medium, chunky, and super bulky. You may have already guessed that fine is the thinnest and super bulky the fattest.

The same yarn weights can have different names:

Fine — sport weight

Light — DK or light worsted

Medium — worsted

Chunky — craft or rug

Super Bulky — bulky

You can learn more about yarn weights on page 20.

When you're first learning to crochet, it's best to use a light-colored, thicker yarn—medium (worsted), chunky, or super bulky weight—that has a smooth texture, and a size H (5mm) or I (5.5mm) hook. The light color, larger hook, and thicker yarn makes it easier to see the stitches as you make them. As you get more comfortable holding the yarn and working the stitches, you'll be able to work with any size hook and yarn.

Sometimes you hold two strands of yarn together and crochet them as one. One of the most common reasons for doing this is to take two thinner yarns and make them into a thicker yarn for your crochet. Another reason is that you can make some neat color combinations by mixing yarn this way.

How to Crochet

Now that you've read about it, it's time to get busy and get crocheting! The illustrations will help you learn what to do.

HOLDING THE YARN

In crochet you hold the yarn in your left hand and work the hook with your right hand (all of this is reversed for left-handed people). You wrap the yarn around your little finger and then your pointer finger, as shown in figure 1, so that you can control the yarn as you make your stitches.

SLIPKNOT AND CHAIN

You begin almost every crochet project by making a slipknot and then a chain. Think of this chain as your "foundation," because your first row of stitches is always made by crocheting into this chain.

Making the Slipknot

1. To make a slipknot, hold the tail of the yarn in your left hand and wrap the yarn around your right pointer finger, as shown in figure 2.

This project was made with the slipknot and chain.

2. Take your finger out of the loop you just made and push a second loop up through the bottom of the first loop, as shown in figure 3.

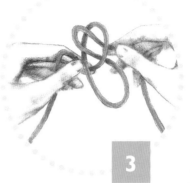

3. Put your hook through the new loop. Hold onto both ends of yarn and pull the knot snugly up to the hook, as shown in figure 4. But not too tight! You want to be able to slide it off the hook later.

Making a Chain (ch)

After making the slipknot, wrap the yarn around the hook once and pull it through the loop on the hook, as shown in figures 5 and 6.

Always wrap the yarn around the hook clockwise—from behind, up, over, and then down in front. You can control the first stitches better if you hold the tail end of the yarn with your left hand while working these beginning steps. Repeat this step for each chain.

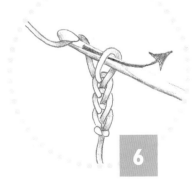

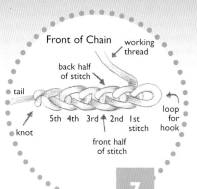

Front of Chain

working thread

back half of stitch

tail

knot

loop for hook

5th 4th 3rd 2nd 1st stitch

front half of stitch

7

Here are the parts of the chain. Figure 7 shows the front of the chain, and figure 8 shows the back. Pay special attention to how the stitches are numbered in the chain. Knowing this will help you when you get to the instructions because they'll tell you which stitch to put the hook into when you begin a row or round.

Look at those stitches!

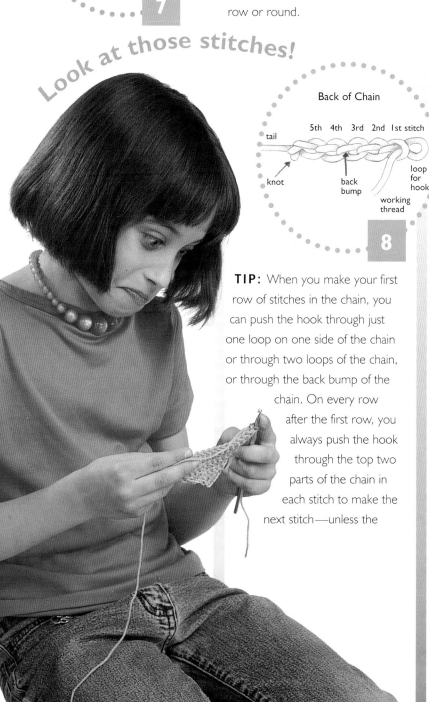

Back of Chain

tail

5th 4th 3rd 2nd 1st stitch

knot

back bump

loop for hook

working thread

8

TIP: When you make your first row of stitches in the chain, you can push the hook through just one loop on one side of the chain or through two loops of the chain, or through the back bump of the chain. On every row after the first row, you always push the hook through the top two parts of the chain in each stitch to make the next stitch—unless the

instructions say to "work in the front half of the stitch" or "work in the back half of the stitch," or when you're working on an advanced stitch like the front post double crochet on page 20.

STITCHES (sts)

When you're learning the stitches, you want to practice until you feel comfortable making them. Don't worry about going too slowly at first, you'll get faster the more you crochet. To practice each stitch, make a slipknot and then a chain of seven or eight stitches before you begin. To help make your stitches even, hold the chain just below or next to where you insert your hook as you make each stitch.

Slip Stitch (sl st)

1. Push the hook through the second chain from the hook, as shown in figure 9. When you do this, you'll have two loops on the hook made of one chain and one loop.

9

2. Wrap the yarn around the hook, known as a yarn over (yo), and pull through both stitches on the hook, as shown in figure 10. After you do that you'll have one loop left on the hook. To continue, push the hook through the next chain and repeat step 2, then repeat this until you come to the end of the row.

Single Crochet (sc)

1. Push the hook through the second chain from the hook, as shown in figure 11. Now you have two loops on the hook made from one chain and one loop.

2. Wrap the yarn around the hook (yo), and pull through the chain only, as shown in figure 12. When you do this, you'll have two loops on the hook.

3. Wrap the yarn around the hook again (yo), and pull through both loops on the hook, as shown in figure 13. You will have one loop on the hook. To continue, push the hook into the next chain and repeat steps 2 and 3. Repeat this until you come to the end of the row.

Half Double Crochet (hdc)

1. Wrap the yarn around the hook (yo), then push the hook through the third chain from the hook, as shown in figure 14. When you do this, you'll have three loops on the hook made from one chain and two loops.

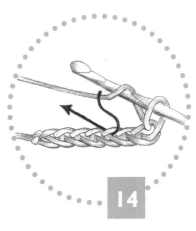

2. Wrap the yarn around the hook (yo), and pull through the chain, as shown in figure 15, leaving you with three loops on the hook.

3. Wrap the yarn around the hook (yo), and pull through all three loops on the hook, as shown in figure 16. You will have one loop on the hook. To continue, repeat steps 1, 2 and 3 working into the next chain. Repeat this until you come to the end of the row.

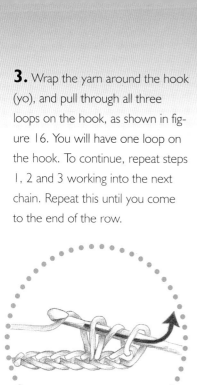

16

Double Crochet (dc)

1. Wrap the yarn around the hook (yo), and push the hook through the fourth chain from the hook, as shown in figure 17. You'll have three loops on the hook made from one chain and two loops.

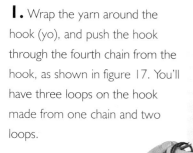

17

2. Wrap the yarn around the hook (yo), and pull it through the chain, as shown in figure 18. Now you'll have three loops on the hook.

18

3. Wrap the yarn around the hook (yo), and pull through two loops on the hook, as shown in figure 19. When you do this, you'll have two loops on the hook.

4. Wrap the yarn around the hook (yo), and pull through the last two loops on the hook, as shown in figure 20. You'll be left with one loop on the hook. To continue, repeat steps 1 to 4 working into the next chain. Repeat this until you come to the end of the row.

19

20

Finishing Off

When you're at the end of a section of crochet or you finish a project, you need to make sure your hard work doesn't unravel! All you need to do is pass the cut end of your yarn through the last loop of your crochet to lock the stitch. It's up to you to always remember to do this. Sometimes crochet instructions will tell you to do this, but most of the time they don't.

BEYOND THE BASICS

ongratulations! You've learned to crochet and want to know more so you can work on other projects. In this section you'll learn about advanced stitches and techniques and get more information about hooks and yarn.

ADVANCED STITCHES

Now that you are familiar with abbreviations, follow the instructions to learn new stitches.

Half Triple Crochet (htr)

Yo twice, hk through 5th ch from hk, yo, pull through ch, yo, pull through all lps on hk.

Triple Crochet (tr)

Yo twice, hk through 5th ch from hk, yo, pull through ch, [yo, pull through 2 lps on hk] three times.

Front Post Double Crochet (fpdc)

Yo, hk behind the post of the st in the row below (the post is the vertical part of the double crochet, below the part you usually crochet into), yo, pull through the post, [yo, pull through 2 lps] twice.

Back Post Double Crochet (bpdc)

Yo, entering from the backside of the crocheting, hk around the post of the st in the row below (the post is the vertical part of the double crochet, below the part you usually crochet into), yo, pull through the post, [yo, pull through 2 lps] twice.

ADVANCED TECHNIQUES

There are many more techniques to learn, but these two will add a lot of new options to your crochet work.

Crocheting Backwards

Single crocheting backwards around the edge of a project creates a textured, undulating finished edge. To crochet backwards, insert the hook into the stitch to the right of the beginning of the yarn.

Wrap the yarn around the hook and pull through the stitch on the hook. Now, wrap the yarn around the hook and pull through both loops on the hook. Be sure to make very loose stitches so they don't pull on the edges of the piece, causing it to pucker.

CHANGING COLORS

When crocheting with more than one color, it helps to understand what's happening to the stitches as you make them. If you change colors for a single crochet stitch, your new color will slant to the left at the top. The last yarn over you pull through the last two loops on the hook actually sits between the stitch just made and the next stitch, causing the slant. The next row of stitches passes through this yarn over, breaking up the color pattern and making it look awkward. Because of this, most of the time you'll need to change to the new yarn color for the last yarn-over of the stitch before the stitch with the new color. Doing this will give your colorwork a much smoother appearance.

HOOKS AND YARN

The information here will help you become even more familiar with hooks and yarn.

Hook Sizes

There are many sizes of crochet hooks and several different companies that make them. Some companies only make the most popular sizes of hooks while some companies some don't always use the same sizing or names. On the right is a chart showing some of the different hook sizes. If you're confused by this, always check the millimeter size that's stamped on the shank of the hook to get the size you need—this size remains constant no matter who makes the hook.

Yarn Sizes or Weights

Yarn comes in many different thicknesses. On the following page are the common names for yarn thickness with a description of them and what size hook you usually use with them.

U. S.	Metric	U. K.
16	0.4mm	
14	0.6mm	
12	0.75mm	
10	1mm	
9	1.25mm	
8	1.4mm	
7	1.5mm	
B/1	2.25mm	
C/2	2.75mm	
D/3	3.25mm	10
E/4	3.5mm	9
F/5	3.75mm	8
G/6	4mm	7
	4.55mm	
H/8	5mm	6
I/9	5.5mm	5
J/10	6mm	4
K	6.5mm	3
	7mm	2
N	9mm	
P	10mm	
Q	16mm	
S	19mm	

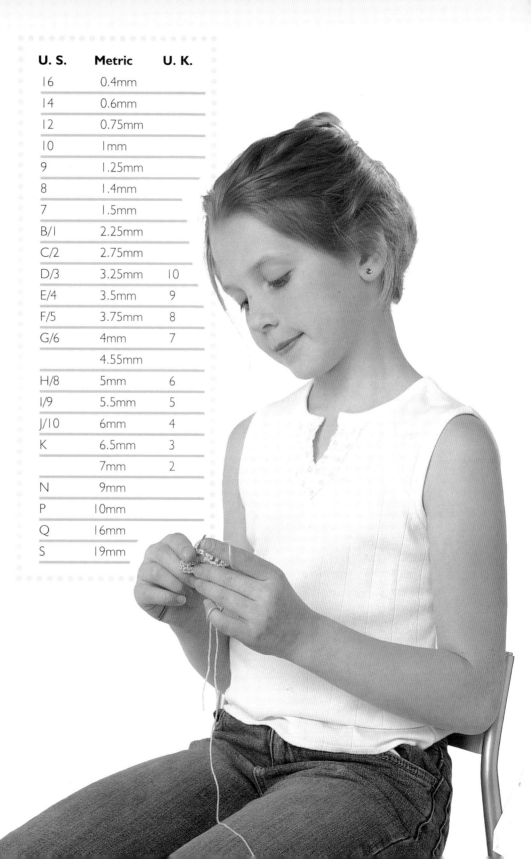

Yarn Weights

Weight	Description	Hook Size
Lace	Threads, very thin yarn	.4 - 2.25 mm 16 - B/I
Fine or fingering	Thin sock yarn, about 1/16 inch thick	2.25 - 3.5 mm B - E
Fine or sport	Traditionally used for baby items and thick socks	3.5 - 4.5 mm E-7
Light or DK	Between sport weight and worsted weight	4.5 - 5.5 mm 7-I
Medium or Worsted	About 1/8 inch thick. This is the most familiar yarn size in the U. S.	5.5 - 6.5 mm I-K
Chunky or Bulky	Thick yarn	6.5 - 9 mm K-P
Super Bulky	Very thick yarn, 1/4 inch or more thick	9 mm - larger P and Larger

Yarn Content

Yarn and thread were once made of natural fibers, such as sheep's wool or cotton. Today you can find dozens of yarn types ranging from all-wool yarn to blended yarns that are made from mixing different types of fibers together. Each fiber (the threads or hairs that make up the yarn) has something special about it that gives the yarn a certain feel or property. For instance, wool can be itchy to some people, but it will also fuzz-up and felt very well in the washer or dryer. Left is a list of yarn types and where they come from.

Where Does Yarn Come From?

Fibers	Sources
Alpaca	Long-necked animal originally from South America (smaller than the llama)
Bamboo	Similar to cotton, made from bamboo plants
Camel	Soft down of camels
Cotton	Cotton plants
Linen	Flax plants
Llama	Long-necked animal originally from South America
Mohair	Airy, hairy yarn from angora goats
Rayon	Made from the cellulose in plant material that is chemically changed into yarn
Silk	Made from the cocoons of silk worms
Synthetic	Man-made fibers including acrylics, polyester, and nylon
Wool	Sheep hair

Yarn Texture

When companies make yarn, they can put little bumps in it, or make it fuzzy or smooth. Many of these characteristics have names. Following is a list of some common names for different textures of yarn.

Boucle
(pronounced boo - CLAY)

This French term meaning "loop" is the name for a yarn with loops that create a bumpy texture in the finished crochet work.

Chenille
(pronounced sha - NEAL)

This is soft fuzzy yarn that looks like velvet. It can be difficult to crochet because the yarn doesn't stretch much and tends to get damaged if you have to pull out any stitches.

Mercerized

This is a process used on cotton to make it smooth and shiny.

Ply

If you take several different pieces of yarn and look at them closely you can see that they are either made up of just one strand of yarn or several smaller strands of yarn twisted together. If it's just one strand of yarn, it's called "single ply," if it has three strands (or plies) it's called "three-ply" yarn, and so on. You can also find yarn that has two or more strands of plied yarn twisted together. Each type of treatment makes the yarn handle and look a little different.

Foreign Names

Crochet terms have different names in the United States than in other parts of the world. All the instructions in this book are written in American terms. The chart below shows some of the most common international terms.

U. S.	European
slip stitch (sl st)	single crochet
single crochet (sc)	double crochet
half double crochet (hdc)	half treble crochet
double crochet (dc)	treble crochet
triple crochet (tr)	double treble crochet
skip (sk)	miss

Slub

A yarn with slubs in it means it has little bumps along the yarn. Sometimes they are the same color as the yarn and sometimes they are different, contrasting colors.

Yarn Colors

There's more to color than you might think. Here are some things to think about when choosing colors of yarn for your projects.

Dye lot

Most yarns have a dye lot number by the color name and number. This means that all the balls of yarn with the same dye lot number were colored at the same time and will have the same exact color. When you buy more than one ball of yarn for a project, you want to make sure all the balls of a color have the same dye lot number, so the color will be the same for the whole project. Blue yarn from company XYZ with dye lot #3

may look a little different from the same company's blue yarn from dye lot #4.

Solid

This one's pretty obvious. The yarn is all one color.

Space Dyed

This is a type of variegated yarn where there is a section of yarn that is one color, usually for several inches, and then the yarn is a different color for several inches. The yarn will have at least two different colors, but can have many colors as well.

Spot Dyed

This is a type of variegated yarn with spots of color changes that can be an inch in length or less and can be unevenly spaced along the yarn, or at regular places.

Variegated

This is any yarn that varies in color along the yarn, and includes the spaced-dyed and spot-dyed yarn described above.

The Projects
FUN & GAMES!

These simple projects will get you started with crochet. You'll get used to holding the hook and yarn and making the stitches. When you're done, you'll have games to play and some colorful accessories to wear. As you keep practicing, you'll get faster and your stitches will get more and more even. Before you know it, you'll be moving on to make the other great projects in this book!

Shoelaces

Whoever thought shoelaces would become a hot fashion statement? Make them in the colors you want to create your own look. This is a great project for getting used to holding the yarn and hook, and for learning to make chain stitches.

SKILL LEVEL

Easy

FINISHED SIZE

About 56 inches long including tail ends

MATERIALS

- 1 skein of medium-weight yarn in your favorite color
- Size H (5mm) crochet hook
- Tapestry needle

GAUGE

4 chains (ch) = 1"

STITCHES USED

Chain (ch)

INSTRUCTIONS

1. Make a slip knot about 3 inches from the end of the yarn.

2. As shown in figure 1, make a chain (ch) about 50 inches long, which will end up being about 200 stitches (sts) in the gauge. Or, make a chain that is the length you need.

3. When you've made all the chains to get the length, you'll have one loop left on the hook. Cut the yarn about 3 inches from the hook to leave a tail. Now pull the tail through the last loop (lp) to finish off. Don't cut off the tail! Repeat steps 1 to 3 for the other shoelace.

4. Thread the tapestry needle with one tail of the chain, and then thread the chain through your shoes' eye holes.

YARNS USED

- 1 skein of Coats & Clark Yarn's Red Heart Classic, 100% acrylic, 3 1/2 oz/100g, in Olympic Blue #0849.

- 1 skein of Coats & Clark Yarn's Red Heart Classic, 100% acrylic, 3 1/2 oz/100g, in White #0001.

- 1 skein of Caron Wintuk No Dye Lot 100% acrylic, 3 1/2 oz/100g, in Christmas Red #3005.

Picking Up the Pieces

If you're just starting to crochet, you may not have any yarn around the house. But once you get going, you'll notice that little odds and ends of leftover yarn from other projects seem to multiply overnight. Making small projects can help you use up your extra yarn. This project, Shoelaces, is perfect for that. You can make shoelaces in different colors for every day of the week!

String Game

Almost everyone knows at least one string game, like Cat's Cradle or Jacob's Ladder. The great thing about making your own string is that it can be the color and length you want. You could even super-size it, making a game for two people to play.

SKILL LEVEL

Easy

FINISHED SIZE

About 60 inches around

MATERIALS

- 1 skein of medium-weight yarn in your favorite color
- Size H (5mm) crochet hook
- Tapestry needle

GAUGE

4 chains (ch) = 1"

STITCHES USED

Chain (ch)

INSTRUCTIONS

1. Make a slip knot about 3 inches in from the end of the yarn.

2. Make a chain (ch) about 60 inches long, which will be about 200 stitches (sts) in the gauge when stretched out.

3. Cut the yarn about 3 inches from the hook to leave a tail. Now pull the tail through the last loop (lp) to finish off.

4. Tie the tails into a tight square knot to make a continuous chain, as shown in figures 1 and 2.

5. Weave in the ends.

YARN USED

1 skein of Coats & Clark Yarn's Red Heart Classic, 100% acrylic, 3 1/2 oz/100g, in Pumpkin #0254, 1 skein of Coats & Clark Yarn's Red Heart Kids, 100% acrylic, 4oz/113g, in Bikini #2945.

Key Chain

Do your keys get lost in the bottomless pit of your backpack? The tail on the key chain lets you know by touch that you've found them—unless that fuzzy feeling is really last week's sandwich that you forgot to eat! This project starts you off making single crochet stitches in a circle over a metal ring. It's a good way to get familiar with working in the round.

SKILL LEVEL

Easy

FINISHED SIZE

About 2 inches across with a 4-inch tail

MATERIALS

- 1 skein of medium-weight yarn in your favorite color

- Size H (5mm) crochet hook

- 2 metal split rings, one 1 inch across, and the other 1½ inches across

GAUGE

4 single crochet (sc) = 1"

STITCHES USED

Single crochet (sc)

INSTRUCTIONS

1. Slide one split ring onto the other, linking them together. You will be working the stitches on the larger ring.

2. Make a slip knot about 4 inches from the end of the yarn.

3. Slide the hook (hk) into the large ring.

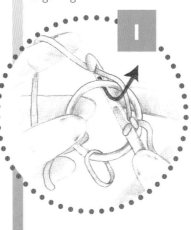

4. Yarn over (yo), and pull yarn through the ring, as shown in figure 1.

5. Yarn over (yo), and pull the yarn through both loops (lps) on the hook (hk), as shown in figure 2.

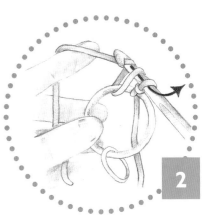

6. Repeat (rep) steps 3 to 5 until you have worked the stitches (sts) all the way around the ring.

7. Cut the yarn to about 4 inches from the ring to leave a tail, and pull it through both loops (lps) left on the hook (hk).

8. Make a fringe. Cut 20 pieces of yarn, each 12 inches long, and fold them in half. Poke the fold up through the large ring, and then push all the ends through the loop formed by the fold. Pull tight so the strands tighten around the 4-inch tail of yarn. Cut the ends so they are all the same length.

YARN USED

1 skein of Coats & Clark Yarn's Red Heart Kids, 100% acrylic, 4 oz/113g, in Bikini #2945.

Circle Games

These handy little circles, crocheted "in the round," can be used for all sorts of games from tick-tack-toe, to checkers (make half of them red and half of them black), to basketball (see how many you can get into a cup or bowl across the table or room), to the target practice game shown.

SKILL LEVEL

Easy

FINISHED SIZE

About 1 1/2 inches across

MATERIALS

- 1 skein of worsted-weight yarn in your favorite color
- Size H (5mm) crochet hook
- 9 x 12-inch sheet of foam
- 1- or 2-inch suction cup
- Self-adhesive hook-and-loop dots
- Markers, paints, or glue to decorate the foam target

GAUGE

4 double crochet (dc) = 1"

STITCHES USED

Chain (ch)

Double crochet (dc)

Slip stitch (sl st)

INSTRUCTIONS

1. Chain 4 (ch 4), turn.

2. Work 13 double crochet (dc) in the 4th chain (ch) from the hook (hk). (Yes, all the stitches are worked in the same chain!) When you're finished, you'll see that your stitches have formed a circle.

3. Join the ends together by making a slip stitch (sl st) in the top of chain (ch) 3, as shown in figure 1.

4. Finish off and weave in the ends.

5. Make five or six circles following steps 1 to 4.

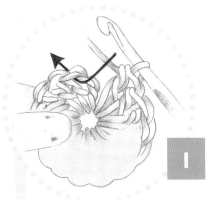

6. You can draw a target on a sheet of foam using markers or paints, and then stick "hook" parts of the hook-and-loop dots onto the foam. If you want to get fancy, cut circles from different colors of foam and then glue them to a sheet of foam. Make a hole in the top of the foam, and attach the suction cup to the back.

7. Stick your foam target pad to a window and have fun getting points when you get the circles to stick to the dots.

Hint: You need to toss the circles lightly from only about 3 feet away. This would be a good travel game in the back seat of a car.

YARN USED

1 skein of Coats & Clark Yarn's Red Heart Kids, 100% acrylic, 5 oz/140g, in Lime #2652.

Scrunchies

T ired of all your old scrunchies? Can't find the right color to wear? Personalize your look by making your own just the way you want! Shown are two versions, one plain and one with ruffles.

SKILL LEVEL

Easy

FINISHED SIZE

About 3 inches across for the plain scrunchy, and 4 inches across for the ruffled version

MATERIALS

- 1 skein of medium-weight yarn in your favorite color
- Size H (5mm) crochet hook
- 1 plain elastic hair band

GAUGE

4 double crochet (dc) = 1"

STITCHES USED

Chain (ch)

Slip stitch (sl st)

Double crochet (dc)

INSTRUCTIONS

1. Make a slip knot about 3 inches from the end of the yarn.

2. Insert the hook (hk) into the hair band.

3. Yarn over (yo), and pull the yarn through the hair band.

4. Yarn over (yo), and pull the yarn through both loops (lps) on the hook (hk).

5. Chain 3 (ch 3).

6. Double crochet (dc) in the hair band. To do this: first yarn over (yo) and insert the hook (hk) into the hair band. Then yarn over (yo) and pull through the hair band. Next, yarn over (yo), and pull the yarn through the 2 loops (lps) on the hook (hk), yarn over (yo) and pull the yarn through the last 2 loops (lps) on the hook (hk) ([yo, pull through 2 lps on the hk] twice.)

7. Repeat (rep) step 6 until you have worked the stitches (sts) all the way around the ring.

8. Slip stitch (sl st) in the top of chain 3 (ch-3) to join the stitches into a circle, as shown in figure 1.

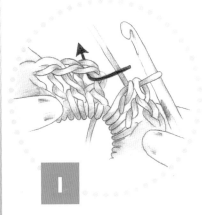

1

9. Cut the yarn, leaving a tail that's about 3 inches long, and pull it through the last loop (lp). Weave in the end.

Now try it a different way! To make a ruffled scrunchy, work through step 8 above, then continue as follows:

10. Chain (ch 3), and then work 3 double crochet (dc) in the next stitch (st).

11. Now work 4 double crochet (dc) in the next stitch (st), as shown in figure 2.

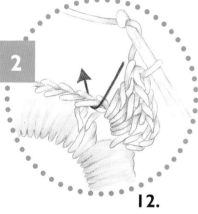

12. Repeat (rep) step 11 for each stitch (st) around.

13. Slip stitch (sl st) in the top of chain 3 (ch-3) to join the stitches into a circle.

14. Cut the yarn to leave a tail about 3 inches long, and pull it through the last loop (lp) then weave in the end.

YARN USED

1 skein of Coats & Clark Yarn's Red Heart Kids, 100% acrylic, 4 oz/113g, in Beach #2940.

SHAPE UP !

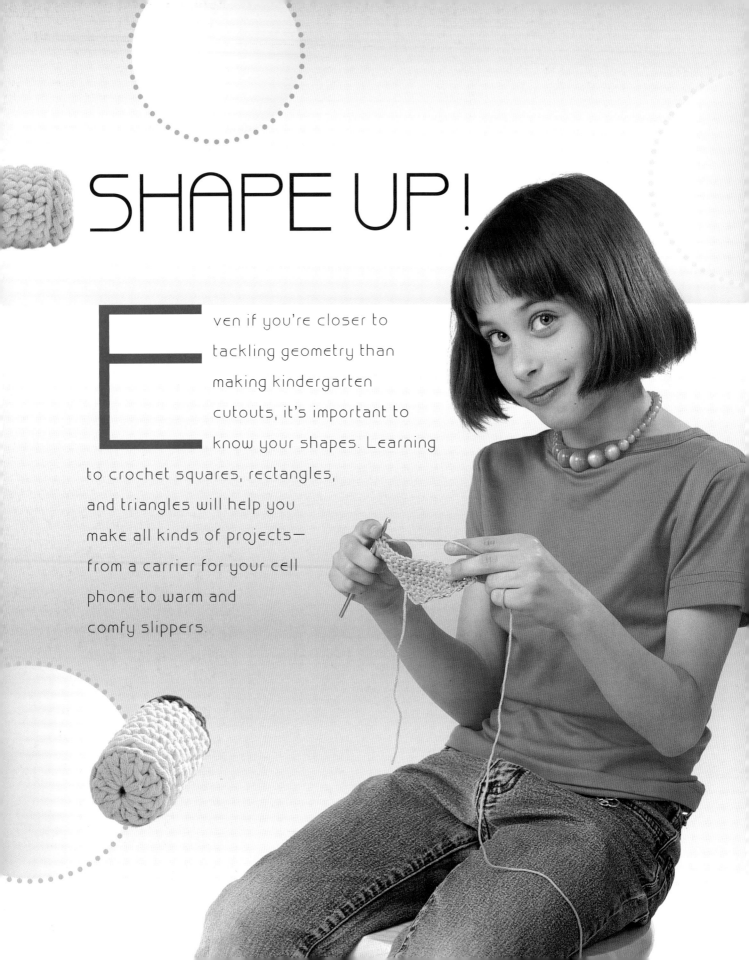

Even if you're closer to tackling geometry than making kindergarten cutouts, it's important to know your shapes. Learning to crochet squares, rectangles, and triangles will help you make all kinds of projects—from a carrier for your cell phone to warm and comfy slippers.

Comfy Slippers

Even when you're chillin' you can have warm feet. The secret to shaping these slippers, made from simple crocheted rectangles, is the bottoms you sew on later. They're suede on the outside, warm and woolly on the inside, and have holes along their edges that make them easy to sew onto the crochet. (You can get the bottoms through mail order or at many specialty yarn stores.)

SKILL LEVEL

Easy

FINISHED SIZE (ACCORDING TO YOUR SHOE SIZE)

Child's 1–4, (Child's size 5–10, Child's size 11–Women's size 5, Women's size 6–10, Men's size 9–12)

FINISHED SIZE (ACCORDING TO THE LENGTH OF YOUR SHOE BOTTOM)

4-5 inches (6–7, 8–9, 9–10, 11–12 inches)

MATERIALS

- 2 skeins each in red and black lightweight sport-weight yarn, or 2 skeins of a red-and-black variegated medium worsted-weight yarn
- 1 pair of fleece-lined slipper bottoms
- Size H (5mm) crochet hook
- Tapestry needle
- Safety pins
- 2 buttons

Sizing It Up

This is the only project in the book that has different sizes in the instructions. Most clothing instructions are set up this same way. The first number is for the smallest size, and the other numbers in parentheses are for the other sizes, in order, from second smallest to largest. To follow the instructions, find your shoe size under Finished Size. You can also measure the bottom of your shoe and make your slippers according to that size. Once you know the size you're going to make, only pay attention to the numbers in that location in the instructions. Some people like to photocopy the instructions and then use a highlighter to mark the size they will be making throughout the instructions.

GAUGE

14 sts = 4"

15 rows = 4"

STITCHES USED

Chain (ch)

Single crochet (sc)

SPECIAL NOTE

These slippers were made by holding two strands of yarn together, one black and one red, and crocheting them as one.

INSTRUCTIONS

RECTANGLES (MAKE TWO)

Foundation: Chain 6 (8, 9, 11, 12) turn.

Row 1: Chain 1 (ch 1), single crochet (sc) in second chain (ch) from hook (hk) and in each chain (ea ch) across, turn. You will now have 6 (8, 9, 11, 12) stitches (sts) total.

Row 2: Chain 1 (ch 1), single crochet (sc) in each stitch (ea st) across, turn.

Repeat row 2 until the crochet work is 9 inches (13, 17, 20, 23 inches) long. Weave in the ends.

ASSEMBLY

As shown in figure 1, overlap the left end over the right end of one rectangle. This will become the toe of the slipper; the other end will be the heel. Use safety pins to pin a shoe bottom to the slipper. Pin it to the center of the toe (at the center of the overlapping ends) and at the center of the heel.

As shown in figure 2, use a 60-inch length of yarn to stitch the crocheted slipper top to the bottom. Use the simple buttonhole stitch—

the drawing shows you how to make it. Begin by stitching through both layers of crochet formed by overlapping the rectangle for the toe section, and then stitch all along one side to the heel and back up the other side to the toe. Remove the safety pins.

Weave in the ends. Repeat the process for the other slipper, but this time overlap the right end over the left. Try on the slippers and pin the top two layers together where you want the button to be. Walk around a little to make sure it's up far enough to hold the slippers on your feet. Then make sure you can get them on and off easily. Sew the button in place through both layers where you placed the pin. Remove the pin.

YARN USED

2 skeins of Dale of Norway Yarn's *Tiur*, 60% mohair, 40% pure new wool, 1 3/4 oz/50g, 126yd/115m, in color #4027

2 skeins of Berroco Yarns' *Sensuwool*, 80% wool, 20% nylon, 1 3/4 oz/50g, 90yd/82m, in Black #6334

Juggling Blocks

aking these three blocks gives you practice in decreasing, crocheting around the edges of crochet work, and stitching shapes together. But why be practical? When you're finished you can begin your new career as a circus juggler!

SKILL LEVEL

Intermediate

FINISHED SIZE

Approximately 2 to 3 inches

MATERIALS

- 1 skein each of chunky, bulky weight yarn in blue, green, yellow, and purple
- Size I (5.5mm) crochet hook
- Tapestry needle
- Stuffing

GAUGE

10 sts = 4"

12 rows = 4"

STITCHES USED

Chain (ch)

Single crochet (sc)

Double crochet (dc)

INSTRUCTIONS

CUBE

One Square

Foundation: Using the blue yarn, chain 5 (ch 5), turn.

Row 1: Chain 1 (ch 1), single crochet (sc) in 2nd chain (ch) from hook (hk) and each chain (ea ch) across, turn. You will now have 5 stitches (5 sts total).

Rows 2-4: Chain 1 (ch 1), single crochet (sc) in each stitch (ea st) across, turn.

Row 5 and border: Figure 1 will show you how following the instructions for this row will shape your square. Chain 1 (ch 1), then make 4 single crochet (4 sc), across the top, continuing around the edge of the crocheting, make 3 single crochet (3 sc) along the left side, 3 single crochet (3 sc) in the corner, 3 single crochet (3 sc) along the bottom, 3 single crochet (3 sc) in the corner, 3 single crochet (3 sc) along the right side, 2 single crochet (2 sc) in the top right corner.

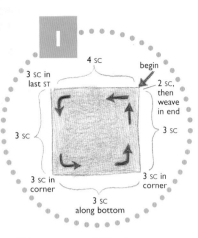

Weave in end. Make five more squares, two purple, one more blue, one green, and one yellow, for a total of six squares. Sew the squares together, and add stuffing before closing the cube up along the last edge.

CYLINDER

Foundation: Using the purple yarn, chain (ch) 4, turn.

Row 1: 12 double crochet (dc) in 4th chain (ch) from hook (hk), slip stitch (sl st) in top of chain 4 (ch-4).

Changing colors to the yellow yarn, pull the yellow yarn through last half of stitch (st), do not turn. Figure 2 shows how you will

change colors once you make one end of the cylinder. The yellow yarn will form the sides as you work around and around.

Round 2: Single crochet (sc) in the back half of each stitch (ea st) around, do not turn.

Rounds 3–8: Single crochet (sc) in each stitch (ea st) around. Cut yarn to leave a 10-inch end and pull it through last loop. Set aside.

Using the green yarn, make the foundation and row 1 as you did with the purple yarn, then weave in the end. This will become the other end of your cylinder. Stuff the cylinder and sew the green end to the yellow opening with the 10 inches of yellow yarn.

PYRAMID

One Triangle

Foundation: Using the green yarn, chain 5 (ch 5), turn.

Row 1: Chain 1 (ch 1), single crochet (sc) in 2nd chain (ch) from hook (hk) and each chain (ea ch) across, turn. You will have 5 stitches (5 sts total).

Row 2: Chain 1 (ch 1), skip 1 (sk1), 4 single crochet (4 sc), turn. You will have 4 stitches (4 sts total).

Row 3: Chain 1 (ch 1), skip 1 (sk 1), 3 single crochet (3 sc), turn. You will have 3 stitches (3 sts total).

Row 4: Chain 1 (ch 1), skip 1 (sk 1), 2 single crochet (2 sc), turn. You will have 2 stitches (2 sts total).

Row 5 and border: Figure 3 will show you how following the instructions for this row will shape the border of your triangle. Chain 1 (ch 1), skip 1 (sk 1), 3 single crochet (3 sc) in the next stitch, continuing around the edge of the crocheting, 3 single crochet (3 sc) along the left side, 3 single crochet (3 sc) in the corner, 3 single crochet (3 sc) along the bottom, 3 single crochet (3 sc) in the corner, 4 single crochet (4 sc) along the right side, 3 single crochet (3 sc) in the top corner.

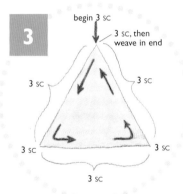

Weave in the end. Make three more triangles so you have one in each color. Make one green square, following the instructions for making one square for the cube above. Sew the triangles together, add stuffing, and then sew the square to the bottom opening.

YARN USED

4 skeins of GGH Yarns' 50% cotton/50% acrylic, 1³⁄₄ oz/50g, 66yd/60m, one skein each in Yellow #05, Green #38, Blue #25, and Purple #37.

Purse

Dressing up or dressing down? Taking this purse from dressy to casual all depends on the type of yarn and button you use. You could also use a thicker yarn and larger hook to make a bigger shoulder bag using the same pattern.

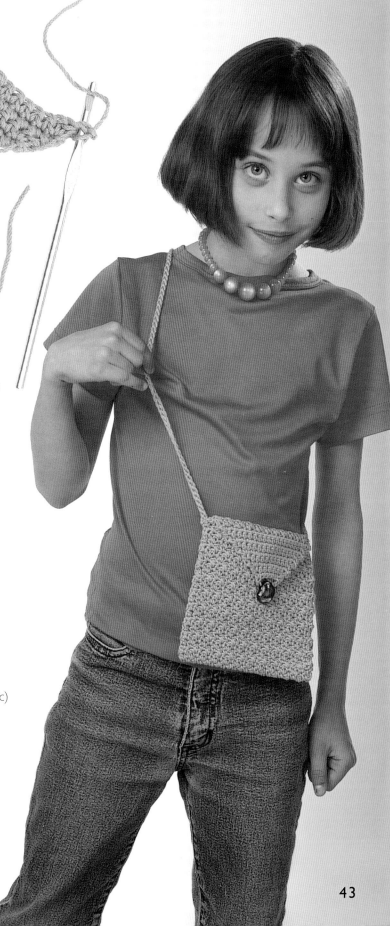

SKILL LEVEL

Intermediate

FINISHED SIZE

About 3 1/2 x 6 inches with a 38-inch-long strap

MATERIALS

- 1 skein of lightweight DK or sport-weight cotton yarn in gold
- Size G (4mm) crochet hook
- Tapestry needle
- 1-inch button
- Steam Iron
- Spray starch

GAUGE

17 sts = 4"

22 rows = 4"

STITCHES USED

Chain (ch)

Single crochet (sc)

Half double crochet (hdc)

Double crochet (dc)

43

INSTRUCTIONS

BODY OF PURSE

Button loop: Chain 12 (ch 12), slip stitch in 1st chain (sl st in 1st ch), forming a circle, turn. Figure 1 shows how to do this.

Row 1: Chain 1 (ch 1), single crochet in next 6 chains (sc in next 6 ch), turn.

Rows 2-9: Chain 2 (ch 2), single crochet in second chain from the hook (sc in 2nd ch from hk), single crochet in each stitch (sc in ea st) across to the last stitch (st), then single crochet and half double crochet in the last stitch ([sc, hdc] in the last st), turn. You will have 22 stitches at the end of row 9.

Row 10: Chain 2 (ch 2), single crochet in the next stitch, double crochet in the next stitch. Repeat the pattern 11 times ([sc, dc] 11 times), turn. You will now have 22 stitches (22 sts total).

Repeat (rep) row 10 until crochet work measures 13 1/2 inches long from row 1. Weave in the end.

STRAP

Foundation: Begin with an 8-inch end. (This will be used later to sew the strap to the bag.) Chain 160 (ch 160), turn.

Row 1: Slip stitch in the back half of each stitch (sl st in the back half of ea st), cut the yarn, leaving an 8-inch end, pull the end through the last stitch (st).

ASSEMBLY

As shown in figure 2, fold the straight end of the bag up 4 1/2 inches and the top flap down just beyond the last row of single crochet.

With an adult present, use the iron with steam to go over the folds you made to set them. Once you have the fold lines, use the iron and spray starch to make the crochet stiffer to help the purse keep its shape. Sew the side seams together, and then sew the strap ends to each side of the bag with their 8-inch ends. Sew the button to the front of the bag where the point of the flap sits when closed.

YARN USED

1 skein of El. D. Mouzakis Yarns' *Butterfly* DK yarn, 100% mercerized cotton, 1 3/4 oz/50g, 108 yd/100m, in Gold #3356

4 1/2"

Pencil Case

Can't find your lucky pencil? You know, the one that helped you ace the last three math quizzes? This small pencil case will store your favorite writing tools in the front of your ring binder where they'll never get lost. So don't sweat getting organized, but good luck on that quiz!

SKILL LEVEL

Intermediate

FINISHED SIZE

About 3 x 6 inches

MATERIALS

- 1 skein each of lightweight DK or sport-weight cotton yarn in gold, orange, and red-orange
- Size F (3.75mm) crochet hook
- Tapestry needle
- Steam iron
- Spray starch
- Plastic straw

GAUGE

18 sts = 4"

22 rows = 4"

STITCHES USED

Chain (ch)

Single crochet (sc)

INSTRUCTIONS

PENCIL HOLDER

Foundation: Using the orange yarn, chain 30 (ch 30), turn.

Row 1: Chain 1 (ch 1), single crochet (sc) in second chain (ch) from the hook (hk) and in each chain (ea ch) across, turn. You will have 30 stitches (30 sts total).

Row 2: Chain 1 (ch 1), single crochet in each stitch across (sc in ea st across), turn.

Rows 3–8: Repeat row 2 (rep row 2).

Change to gold, work even for 4 rows.

Change to red-orange, work even for 14 rows.

Work 4 more rows over the first 15 stitches (sts).

Weave in the end.

ASSEMBLY

Following figure 1, fold the crochet work in half. Attach the orange yarn to the last stitch (st) completed. Working along the side, chain 1 and single crochet in the next 3 stitches (ch 1 and sc in the next 3 sts). To attach the two layers, work at the edge of the crochet work, single crochet (sc) along the side edge through both layers making 1 single crochet in the end of each row (1 sc in the end of ea row). Make 3 single crochet (3 sc) in the corner, and working along the bottom edge, single crochet in each stitch across (sc in ea st across). Weave in the end.

1

Fold in half

sc through both thicknesses

3 sc in corner

sc through both thicknesses

MAKING THE FLAP WITH THE BINDER-HOLES

Attach the red-orange yarn at the top left corner of the holder. Chain 1 (ch 1), single crochet in the next 5 stitches (sc in the next 5 sts), chain 1 (ch 1), skip 1 (sk 1), single crochet in each stitch to the last 4 stitches along the side (sc in ea st to the last 4 sts along the side), chain 1 (ch 1), skip 1 (sk 1, single crochet in the last 3 stitches (sc in the last 3 sts), turn.

Row 2: Chain 1 (ch 1), single crochet in each stitch and chain across (sc in ea st and ch across), turn.

Row 3: Chain 1 (ch 1), single crochet in each st across (sc in ea st across). Weave in the end.

With an adult present, spray the crochet work with the starch and steam press it until it's almost dry. Cut two 1-inch lengths from the straw and wiggle them into the holes you made in the flap by skipping stitches. You may need to stretch the crochet work a little to get the straws to fit in the holes. Let dry completely.

YARN USED

2 skeins of Tahki Imports Ltd. Yarns' *Cotton Classic*, 100% mercerized cotton, 4 1/2 oz/125g, 252yd/230m, one skein each in Rust #3407, and Caramel #3356

1 skein of El. D. Mouzakis Yarns' *Butterfly* DK yarn, 100% mercerized cotton,

1 3/4 oz/50g, 108yd/100m, in Gold #3356

Phone Carrier

Y ou finally got your parents to get you a cell phone? How cool are you! Now if you could only find it. Here's a handy crocheted carrier that will make it easy to catch those calls. Add some beads for even more pizzazz.

SKILL LEVEL

Intermediate

FINISHED SIZE

About 3 x 5 inches

MATERIALS

- 1 cone of nylon crochet cord
- Size F (3.75mm) crochet hook
- Tapestry needle
- Decorative beads with holes large enough to thread onto the nylon crochet cord

GAUGE

17 sts = 4"

12 rows = 4"

STITCHES USED

Chain (ch)

Single crochet (sc)

Double crochet (dc)

INSTRUCTIONS

MAKING THE BODY (BEGINNING AT THE TOP FRONT OPENING)

Foundation: Chain 12 (ch 12), turn.

Row 1: Chain 3 (ch 3), double crochet in the 4th chain from the hook and each chain across (dc in 4th ch from hk and ea ch across), turn. You will have 12 stitches (12 sts total).

Row 2: Chain 1 (ch 1), single crochet in each stitch across (sc in ea st across), turn.

Row 3: Chain 3 (ch 3), double crochet in each stitch across (dc in ea st across), turn.

Repeat (rep) rows 2 and 3, 14 more times.

Repeat (rep) row 2.

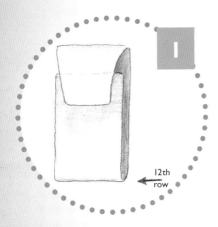

1

12th
row

MAKING THE FLAP

At the beginning of the next row: Chain 3, skip 1, double crochet in each st across, (ch 3, sk 1, dc in ea st across), turn. You will have 11 stitches (11 sts total).

At the beginning of the next row: Chain 1, skip 1, single crochet in each stitch across (ch 1, sk 1, sc in ea st across), turn. You will have 10 stitches (10 sts total).

Repeat each of these two rows one time. You will have 9 stitches, then 8 stitches (9 and 8 sts total). Then work even in the pattern for 2 rows.

ASSEMBLY

As shown in figure 1, fold the bottom of the crochet work up along the 12th row from the beginning. Pin in place.

Work single crochet (sc) along the side edge, working through both layers of crochet to attach them.

When you come to the fold, weave in the end. Begin a new length of cord and single crochet (sc) along the other side edge, working through both layers of crochet. When you come to the top opening, weave in the ends.

Making the Belt Casing

(to fit a belt up to 1-inch-wide)

Foundation: Chain 8 (ch 8), turn.

Row 1: Chain 1 (ch 1), single crochet in the 2nd chain from the hook and each chain across (sc in the 2nd ch from hk and ea ch across), turn.

Rows 2–16: Chain 1, single crochet in each stitch across (ch 1, sc in ea st across), turn.

Weave in the end.

As shown in figure 2, sew the long edges of the casing to the back of the phone case along the 8th row from the top of the flap and the 13th row from the top of the flap on the back side of the phone case.

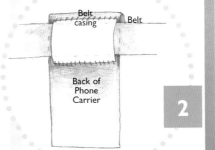

Belt
casing   Belt

Back of
Phone
Carrier

2

ADDING BEADS

Cut a 6-inch length of cord, and tie a knot at one end. String on decorative beads until you have about 1 to 1 1/2 inches of beads. Thread the end of the cord through the center of the flap's edge. String more beads on this end until you have about 1 to 1 1/2 inches of beads. Tie a knot close to the last bead, and cut the cord near the knot.

YARN USED

1 cone of Coats & Clark Yarn's *J. P. Coats Crochet Nylon*, 100% nylon, 150yd/137m, in Black #19

GETTING AROUND

This is one time going around and around in circles won't make you dizzy. Learning to work crochet in the round opens all kinds of possibilities. In this section you'll learn about increasing and decreasing for shaping your projects. Just a heads up—Space Balls on page 58 will be the first project to use all abbreviations.

Large Ball

Take it outside! Getting tired of hearing Mom telling you to go outside to play ball? It'll be a slam-dunk convincing Mom that this very soft ball won't do too much damage if it misses its mark.

SKILL LEVEL

Intermediate

FINISHED SIZE

About 8 inches in diameter

MATERIALS

- 4 skeins of 192yd/175m superfine fingering-weight yarn
- Size H (5mm) crochet hook
- Stitch marker
- Polyester fiberfill stuffing

GAUGE IN SINGLE CROCHET (SC), HOLDING TWO STRANDS TOGETHER (TOG) AS ONE

4 sts = 1"

STITCHES USED

Single crochet (sc)

INSTRUCTIONS

Foundation: Chain 2 (ch 2), turn.

Round 1: 6 single crochet in the second chain from the hook (6 sc in 2nd ch from hk), place marker (pm), do not turn.

Round 2: 2 single crochet in each stitch around (2 sc in ea st around). Move marker to the last stitch you made. You will have 12 stitches (12 sts total).

Round 3: Single crochet in the next stitch, and then make 2 single crochet in next stitch, do this six times. Move marker to the last stitch you made. When you're done, you'll have 18 stitches. ([SC in next st, 2 sc in next st] 6 times, pm (18 sts total) .)

Round 4: Single crochet in the next 2 stitches, and then make 2 single crochet in the next stitch, do this six times. Move marker to the last stitch you made. When you're done you will have 24 stitches. ([SC in next 2 sts, 2 sc in next st] 6 times, pm (24 sts total) .)

Round 5: Single crochet in the next 3 stitches, and then make 2 single crochet in the next stitch, do this six times. When you're done you will have 30 stitches. ([SC in next 3 sts, 2 SC in next st] 6 times, pm (30 sts total) .)

Continue increasing 6 stitches in each round (6 sts in ea round) until you have 14 single crochet then 2 single crochet in the next stitch for each repeat. When you're done

Thick and Thin

Think this yarn is too thin? If you hold two strands together and crochet as if they're one yarn—surprise—it's just as if you're crocheting with a medium-weight yarn. And, by combining strands of different colors, you can come up with some wild color combinations.

you'll have 96 stitches. (14 sc then 2 sc in the next st for each repeat (96 sts total) .) Work even for 21 rounds.

To Begin Decreasing

Decrease round 1: Skip the next stitch, single crochet in the next 15 stitches, do this 6 times. When you're done you will have 90 stitches. ([Sk the next st, sc in the next 15 sts] 6 times (90 sts total).)

Decrease round 2: Skip the next stitch, single crochet in the next 14 stitches, do this 6 times, when you're done you will have 84 stitches. ([Sk the next st, sc in the next 14 sts] 6 times (84 sts total).)

Decrease round 3: Skip the next stitch, single crochet in the next 13 stitches, do this 6 times, when you're done you will have 78 stitches. ([Sk the next st, sc in the next 13 sts] 6 times (78 sts total).)

Continue decreasing by 6 stitches. Try to evenly space the skipped stitches in each round (6 sts evenly spaced in ea round) until the opening is about 3 inches across. Stuff the ball loosely with the stuffing. Continue decreasing until you have 6 stitches (6 sts) left. Weave in the end.

Yarn Used

4 skeins of Paton Yarn's *Kroy 4 Ply Sock Yarn*, 75% washable wool, 25% nylon, 192yds/175m, in Paint Box #54567

Anyone Seen My Row!

Notice anything in the instructions? When working around and around in crochet, the word "row" is replaced with the word "round." Because you're crocheting in a circle, and you're not turning at the end of the row, you're working "in the round."

Hacky Sack

This hacky sack is just like the ones you buy in the store, only better, since you make it yourself! Crocheting this small ball is similar to making the Large Ball on page 52, except you use thinner cotton yarn and fill the hacky sack with beans instead of stuffing.

SKILL LEVEL

Intermediate

FINISHED SIZE

2 1/2 inches in diameter

MATERIALS

- 1 skein each of lightweight sport-weight cotton yarn in red and burgundy
- Size C (2.75mm) crochet hook
- Tapestry needle
- 1 cup dried beans, such as pinto beans
- Stitch marker

GAUGE

6 sts = 1"

6 rows = 1"

STITCHES USED

Chain (ch)

Single crochet (sc)

INSTRUCTIONS

Foundation: Chain 2 (ch 2), turn.

Round 1: Make 6 single crochet in the second chain from the hook and place a marker, do not turn. (6 sc in 2nd ch from hk, pm, do not turn.)

Round 2: Make 2 single crochet in each stitch around. Move marker to the last stitch you made. When you're finished, you'll have 12 stitches. (2 sc in ea st around, (12 sts total).)

Round 3: Single crochet in the next stitch, then make 2 single crochet in the next stitch. Do this 6 times. Move marker to the last stitch you made. When you're finished, you'll have 18 stitches. ([Sc in next st, 2 sc in next st] 6 times (18 sts total).)

Round 4: Single crochet in the next 2 stitches, then make 2 single crochet in the next stitch. Do this 6 times. Move marker to the last stitch you made. When you're finished, you'll have 24 stitches ([Sc in next 2 sts, 2 sc in next st] 6 times, pm (24 sts total).)

Round 5: Single crochet in the next 3 stitches, then make 2 single crochet in the next stitch. Do this 6 times. Move marker to the last stitch you made. When you're finished, you'll have 30 stitches. ([Sc in next 3 sts, 2 sc in next st] 6 times, pm (30 sts total).)

Round 6: Single crochet in the next 4 stitches, then make 2 single cro-

chet in the next stitch. Do this 6 times. Move marker to the last stitch you made. When you're finished, you'll have 36 stitches. ([Sc in next 4 sts, 2 sc in next st] 6 times, pm (36 sts total).)

Round 7: Single crochet in the next 5 stitches, then make 2 single crochet in the next stitch. Do this 6 times. Move marker to the last stitch you made. When you're finished, you'll have 42 stitches. ([Sc in next 5 sts, 2 sc in next st] 6 times, pm (42 sts total).)

Rounds 8–10: Single crochet in each stitch around, place marker. (Sc in ea st around, pm.)

Round 11: Change to burgundy yarn, single crochet in each stitch around. Place marker. (Sc in ea st around, pm.)

Rounds 12–14: Change to red yarn, single crochet in each stitch around. Place marker. (Sc in ea st around, pm.)

Round 15: Skip the next stitch, and single crochet in the next 6 stitches. Do this 6 times. Place marker. When you're finished, you'll have 36 stitches. ([Sk the next st, sc in next 6 sts] 6 times, pm (36 sts total).)

Round 16: Skip the next stitch, and single crochet in the next 5 stitches. Do this 6 times. When you're finished, you'll have 30 stitches. ([Sk the next st, sc in next 5 sts] 6 times, pm (30 sts total).)

Round 17: Skip the next stitch, single crochet in the next 4 stitches. Do this 6 times. Place marker. When you're finished, you'll have 24 stitches. ([Sk the next st, sc in next 4 sts] 6 times, pm (24 sts total).)

Round 18: Skip the next stitch, single crochet in the next 3 stitches. Do this 6 times. Place marker. When you're finished, you'll have 18 stitches. ([Sk the next st, sc in next 3 sts] 6 times, pm (18 sts total).)

Round 19: Skip the next stitch, single crochet in the next 2 stitches. Do this 6 times. When you're finished, you'll have a total of 12 stitches. ([Sk the next st, sc in next 2 sts] 6 times, pm (12 sts total).)

Stuff the sack loosely with beans.

Round 20: Skip the next stitch, single crochet in the next stitch. Do this 6 times. When you're finished, you'll have 6 stitches. ([Sk the next st, sc in next st] 6 times, pm (6 sts total).)

Weave in the end, closing the opening as you work.

YARN USED

2 skeins Plymouth Yarn's *Wildflower D. K.*, 51% cotton/49% acrylic, 1³/₄oz/50g, 137yd/125m, one skein each in Red #63 and Burgundy #62

Space
Balls

Here's your chance to make a ball-toss game like the ones you see at carnivals. You can choose any theme you want. This uses crocheted planets to toss at a game board painted like outer space. This is the first project to use all abbreviations. If you get stuck, check back on page 9 for the list of abbreviations. Okay, now who knows what I sc in 4 sts means?

SKILL LEVEL

Intermediate

FINISHED SIZE

Varies for each planet, from about 1 to 4 inches in diameter

MATERIALS

- 9 skeins (or leftover skeins) of medium worsted-weight yarn in the colors listed in the instructions to represent the planets

- Size G (4mm) crochet hook

- Tapestry needle

- About 4 cups of dry beans such as pinto beans

- Cardboard, foam core, or thin plywood, glue and paint for the target

GAUGE

18 sts = 4"

18 rows = 4"

STITCHES USED

Chain (ch)

Single crochet (sc)

INSTRUCTIONS

THE PLANETS

MERCURY
(THE ORANGE PLANET)

Foundation: Ch 2, turn.

Round 1: 6 sc in 2nd ch from hk, pm, do not turn.

Round 2: 2 sc in ea st around, pm (12 sts total).

Round 3: [Sc in next st, 2 sc in next st] 6 times, pm (18 sts total).

Rounds 4–6: Sc in ea st around, pm.

Round 7: [Sk 1 st, sc in next 2 sts] 6 times, pm (12 sts total).

Fill ball with beans.

Round 8: [Sk 1 st, sc in next st] 6 times, pm (6 sts total).

Weave in the end, closing the opening.

VENUS (THE PINK PLANET)

Beg the same as for Mercury, increasing until you have [1 sc in 3 sts, 2 sc in the next st] 6 times (30 sts total). Work even for 4 rounds, then begin decreasing [sk the first st, sc in the next 4 sts] 6 times (24 sts total). Continue decreasing 6 times each round, and finish the same as Mercury.

EARTH (THE BLUE/GREEN PLANET)

Work the same as for Venus.

MARS (THE RED PLANET)

Beg the same as Mercury, increasing until you have [1 sc in 2 sts and 2 sc in the next st] 6 times around (24 sts total). Work even for 3 rounds, then begin decreasing [sk the first st, sc in the next 3 sts] 6 times around (18 sts total). Continue decreasing 6 times each round, and finish the same as Mercury.

JUPITER (THE BROWN PLANET)

Beg the same as Mercury, increasing until you have [1 sc in 6 sts, 2 sc in the next st] 6 times (48 sts total). Work even for 6 rounds, then begin decreasing [sk the first st, sc in the next 7 sts] 6 times (42 sts total). Continue decreasing 6 times each round, and finish the same as Mercury.

SATURN (THE TAN PLANET)

Beg the same as Mercury, increasing until you have [1 sc in 4 sts, and 2 sc in the next st] 6 times (36 sts total). Work even for 5 rounds, then begin decreasing [sk the first st, sc in the next 5 sts] 6 times (30 sts total). Continue decreasing 6 times each round, and finish the same as Mercury.

After finishing the ball, make the rings of Saturn by attaching a new length of yarn in one of the sts along the center round of the ball and sc in ea st around the center round, pm, then [sc in next 5 sts, 2 sc in next st] 6 times (42 sts total).

URANUS (THE BLUE PLANET)

Beg the same as Mercury, increasing until you have [1 sc in 4 sts, 2 sc in the next st] 6 times (36 sts total). Work even for 5 rounds, then begin decreasing [sk the first st, sc in the next 5 sts] 6 times (30 sts total). Continue decreasing 6 times each round, and finish the same as Mercury.

NEPTUNE (THE GREEN PLANET)

Work the same as for Uranus.

PLUTO (THE PURPLE PLANET)

Beg the same as Mercury, increasing until you have [1 sc in 2 sts, 2 sc in the next st] 6 times (24 sts total). Work even for 2 rounds, then begin decreasing [sk the first st, sc in the next 3 sts] 6 times (18 sts total). Continue decreasing 6 times each round, and finish the same as Mercury.

THE TARGET

To make the target, first have an adult cut several holes in the board, making them from 2 to 4 inches in diameter. You can randomly space the holes like the game board shown, or you can place them in a line from largest to smallest. Paint the board black, and let it dry. Splatter some white paint onto the surface to make distant stars, and then paint a few planets and shooting stars. Let it dry. Lean your target against a tree, wall, or chair outside, and you're ready to play!

YARN USED

A variety of Coats & Clark Yarn's *Red Heart* yarns including *Classic* and *Kids*

Felted Hat

Remember the time Dad did the wash and shrunk your mom's favorite sweater? Well now you have permission to shrink something on purpose! Crochet this over-sized hat, then shrink it down to size by throwing it in the washer using hot water—it's called felting, and it's easy and fun to do. Make sure to use an all-wool yarn.

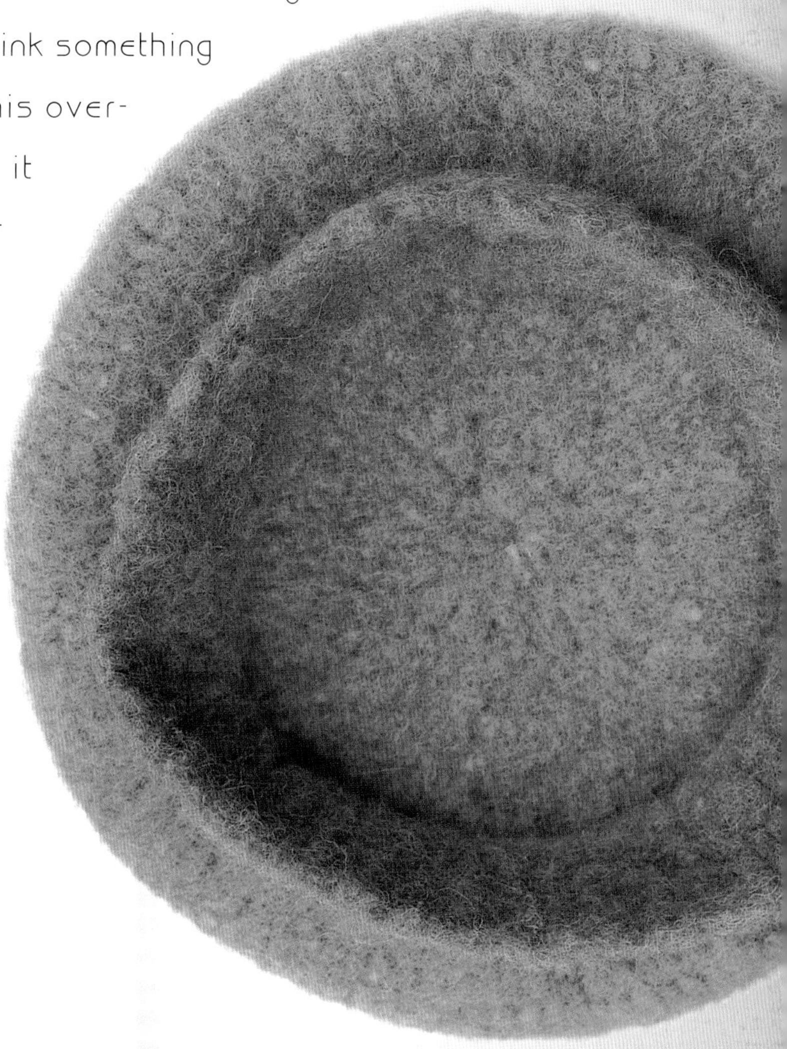

SKILL LEVEL

Intermediate

FINISHED SIZE

20 inches in circumference (this will stretch to fit heads up to 23 inches)

MATERIALS

- 1 skein each of medium worsted-weight non-washable wool yarn in light and dark green
- Size I (5.5mm) crochet hook
- Tapestry needle
- Washing machine

GAUGE

16 sts = 4"

6 rows = 4"

STITCHES USED

Chain (ch)

Single crochet (sc)

Double crochet (dc)

INSTRUCTIONS

BAND

Foundation: Using the dark green yarn, ch 7, turn.

Row 1: Ch 1, sc in 2nd ch from hk and ea ch across, turn (7 sts total).

Rows 2-80: Ch 1, sc in ea st across, turn.

Cut the yarn to 10 inches and pull through the last loop. Thread the 10-inch end of yarn in the tapestry needle and sew the first row to the last row, making a tube shape (be sure the band isn't twisted before you sew it together). Set the band aside until you finish the hat.

HAT (BEGINNING AT THE MIDDLE OF THE TOP, TURNING CH COUNTS AS A ST)

Row 1: Using the light green yarn, ch 4, 14 dc in 4th ch from hk, sl st in top of ch-4.

Row 2: Ch 3, dc in 1st st, 2 dc in ea st around, sl st in top of ch-3 (30 sts total).

Row 3: Ch 3, [dc in next st, 2 dc in next st] rep to last 2 sts, 2 dc, sl st in top of ch-3 (45 sts total).

Row 4: Ch 3, [dc in next 2 sts, 2 dc in next st] rep to last 3 sts, 3 dc, sl st in top of ch-3 (60 sts total).

Row 5: Ch 3, [dc in next 3 sts, 2 dc in next st] rep to last 4 sts, 4 dc, sl st in top of ch-3 (75 sts total).

Rows 6–9: Rep pat, increasing 15 sts ea row (90, 105, 120, 135 sts total).

Rows 10-12: Work even.

Row 13: Ch 3, [8 dc, sk 1] rep around, sl st in top of ch-3 (120 sts total).

Row 14: Ch 3, [7 dc, sk 1] rep around, sl st in top of ch-3 (105 sts total).

Row 15: Ch 3, [6 dc, sk 1] rep around, sl st in top of ch-3 (90 sts total).

Cut yarn to 24 inches and pull through the last loop.

ASSEMBLY

Thread the yarn end in the tapestry needle and sew the hat to the band, making a stitch through each row on the band and skipping every 9th row on the hat. Weave in the ends.

FELTING

Set the washer on hot wash, cold rinse at the lowest water level. Put in about 1 tablespoon of liquid dish soap. Then throw your big hat in and wash it. If the hat hasn't shrunk enough and gotten fuzzy after one cycle, put it through another cycle. Shape it to fit your head, then set it aside to dry in a warm, dry place.

YARN USED

2 skeins of Tahki Imports Ltd. Yarns' *Donegal Tweed*, 100% pure new wool, 3 1/2 oz/100g, 183yd/169m, one skein each in Medium Green #807 and Grass Green #803

What's felting?

Felting is when wool fibers rub against each other until they become matted and stuck together. When this happens, the finished item gets smaller and thicker as the yarn locks together. This makes a solid fabric with little stretch. To make the fibers lock into place, you wash your crocheting in hot water. This causes tiny little hairs on the yarn to relax, open, and spread apart. They mingle and tangle and get caught up with the other hairs in the yarn. When you rinse the crochet in cold water, the hairs pull down tight against the yarn, causing everything to mat and hold together. You can control how much your hat felts by taking it out and checking it every 5 or 10 minutes to see if it's shrunk enough.

Roly Poly Pig

With no feeding, no mess, and no care, this is one pet everyone in the family could love. This huggable guy could be a gift for someone special, or be your own new friend who'll hang out in your room. Plus, he'll have his own personality created especially by you.

SKILL LEVEL

Advanced Intermediate

FINISHED SIZE

About 12 inches long, 10 inches tall, and 20 inches around

MATERIALS

- 2 skeins of medium worsted-weight yarn in light pink
- Size H (5mm) crochet hook
- Tapestry needle
- Polyester fiberfill stuffing
- Small amount of dark pink yarn for face embroidery

GAUGE

16 sts = 4"

16 rows = 4"

STITCHES USED

Chain (ch)

Single crochet (sc)

Double crochet (dc)

Slip stitch (sl st)

INSTRUCTIONS

BODY

Foundation: Ch 2, turn.

Row 1: 6 sc in 2nd ch from hk, pm, do not turn.

Round 2: 2 sc in ea st around, pm (12 sts total).

Increase round 3: (Sc in next st, 2 sc in next st) 6 times, pm (18 sts total).

Increase round 4: (Sc in next 2 sts, 2 sc in next st) 6 times, pm (24 sts total).

Increase round 5: (Sc in next 3 sts, 2 sc in next st) 6 times, pm (30 sts total).

Increase round 6: (Sc in next 4 sts, 2 sc in next st) 6 times, pm (36 sts total).

Increase round 7: (Sc in next 5 sts, 2 sc in next st) 6 times, pm (42 sts total).

Increase round 8: (Sc in next 6 sts, 2 sc in next st) 6 times, pm (48 sts total).

Increase round 9: (Sc in next 7 sts, 2 sc in next st) 6 times, pm (54 sts total).

Increase round 10: (Sc in next 8 sts, 2 sc in next st) 6 times, pm (60 sts total).

Increase round 11: (Sc in next 9 sts, 2 sc in next st) 6 times, pm (66 sts total).

Increase round 12: (Sc in next 10 sts, 2 sc in next st) 6 times, pm (72 sts total).

Increase round 13: (Sc in next 11 sts, 2 sc in next st) 6 times, pm (78 sts total).

Increase round 14: (Sc in next 12 sts, 2 sc in next st) 6 times, pm (84 sts total).

Increase round 15: (Sc in next 13 sts, 2 sc in next st) 6 times, pm (90 sts total).

Increase round 16: (Sc in next 14 sts, 2 sc in next st) 6 times, pm (96 sts total).

Rounds 17–29: Sc in ea st around.

Decrease round 30: (Sk the next st, sc in next 15 sts) 6 times, pm (90 sts total).

Decrease round 31: (Sk the next st, sc in next 14 sts) 6 times, pm (84 sts total).

Decrease round 32: (Sk the next st, sc in next 13 sts) 6 times, pm (78 sts total).

Decrease round 33: (Sk the next st, sc in next 12 sts) 6 times, pm (72 sts total).

Decrease round 34: (Sk the next st, sc in next 11 sts) 6 times, pm (66 sts total).

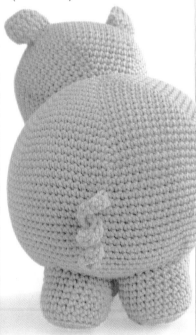

Decrease round 35: (Sk the next st, sc in next 10 sts) 6 times, pm (60 sts total).

Decrease round 36: (Sk the next st, sc in next 9 sts) 6 times, pm (54 sts total).

Stuff the body with fiberfill.

Decrease round 37: (Sk the next st, sc in next 8 sts) 6 times, pm (48 sts total).

Decrease round 38: (Sk the next st, sc in next 7 sts) 6 times, pm (42 sts total).

Decrease round 39: (Sk the next st, sc in next 6 sts) 6 times, pm (36 sts total).

Decrease round 40: (Sk the next st, sc in next 5 sts) 6 times, pm (30 sts total).

Decrease round 41: (Sk the next st, sc in next 4 sts) 6 times, pm (24 sts total).

Decrease round 42: (Sk the next st, sc in next 3 sts) 6 times, pm (18 sts total).

Decrease round 43: (Sk the next st, sc in next 2 sts) 6 times, pm (12 sts total).

Cut the yarn to 8 inches and weave in the end, closing the hole as you finish.

Legs (make four)

Foundation: Ch 4, turn.

Row 1: 11 dc in 4th ch from hk, join to top of ch-3 with sl st (11 sts and one ch-3).

Row 2: Ch 1, 2 sc in ea st around, sl st in ch 1 (24 sts total).

Round 3: Pm, sc in back half of ea st around.

Rounds 4–9: Sc in ea st around, pm.

Cut the yarn to about 12 inches and pull the end through the last loop, stuff the leg with fiberfill, set aside.

Tail

Foundation: Ch 36, turn.

Row 1: Ch 1, hk through back half of 2nd ch from hk, yo, pull through ch, hk through back half of next ch, yo, pull through ch, yo, pull through all three lps on hk, ([hk through back half of next ch, yo, pull through ch] twice, yo, pull through all three lps on hk) repeat across.

Cut yarn to 8 inches, and pull the end through last lp, set aside.

HEAD
(BEGINNING AT THE SNOUT)

Foundation: Ch 4, turn.

Row 1: 11 dc in 4th ch from hk, join to top of ch-3 with sl st (11 sts and one ch-3).

Row 2: Ch 1, 2 sc in ea st around, sl st in ch-1 (24 sts total).

Round 3: Pm, sc in back half of ea st around.

Rounds 4–6: Sc in ea st around, pm.

Increase round 7: 2 sc in ea st around, pm (48 sts total).

Increase round 8: (Sc in next 7 sts, 2 sc in next st) 6 times, pm (54 sts total).

Increase round 9: (Sc in next 8 sts, 2 sc in next st) 6 times, pm (60 sts total).

Increase round 10: (Sc in next 9 sts, 2 sc in next st) 6 times, pm (66 sts total).

Rounds 11–15: Sc in ea st around, pm.

Decrease round 16: (Sk next st, sc in next 10 sts) 6 times, pm (60 sts total).

Decrease round 17: (Sk next st, sc in next 9 sts) 6 times, pm (54 sts total).

Decrease round 18: (Sk next st, sc in next 8 sts) 6 times, pm (48 sts total).

Decrease round 19: (Sk next st, sc in next 7 sts) 6 times, pm (42 sts total).

Decrease round 20: (Sk next st, sc in next 6 sts) 6 times, pm (36 sts total).

Decrease round 21: (Sk next st, sc in next 5 sts) 6 times, pm (30 sts total).

Stuff the head and snout with the fiberfill.

Decrease Round 22: (Sk next st, sc in next 4 sts) 6 times, pm (24 sts total).

Decrease Round 23: (Sk next st, sc in next 3 sts) 6 times, pm (18 sts total).

Decrease Round 24: (Sk next st, sc in next 2 sts) 6 times, pm (12 sts total).

Cut the yarn to 12 inches and thread the end on a tapestry needle. Weave in the end, closing the hole.

EAR (MAKE TWO)

Foundation: Beginning with a 12-inch tail (you'll use this to sew the ear to the head), ch 6, turn.

Row 1: Ch 3, dc in 4th ch from hk and ea ch across, turn (6 sts total).

Row 2: Ch 3, dc in ea st across, turn.

Row 3: Ch 4, [yo twice, hk through next st, yo, pull through st, yo, pull through 2 lps on hk, yo, pull through 2 lps on hk] 6 times, working the last repeat in the top of the ch-3, yo, pull through all 7 lps on hk, yo, pull through lp on hk.

Weave in the working end of yarn and leave the 12-inch end of yarn for stitching. Set aside.

ASSEMBLY

Sew the legs to the bottom of the body, with the front and back legs almost touching each other (leave about 1/2 inch of space between each pair). Sew the tail to the middle of the body behind the back pair of legs, and the head on the opposite side. Sew the ears in a semicircle, about 2 1/2 inches apart and about 4 inches from the center of the nose. Using the dark pink yarn, make the nostrils on the nose with about 5 straight stitches each, and the eyes in the same way only using smaller stitches.

YARN USED

3 skeins Coats & Clark Yarn's *Red Heart Classic*, 100% acrylic, 3 1/2 oz/100g, 198yd/181m), 2 skeins of Light Pink #0737 and 1 skein of Dark Pink #0730

NETWORK!

If you can make a chain and single crochet, you're on your way to crocheting net. You can work back and forth or in the round to make bags, shawls, and scarves—even a shelf for your room!

Corner Shelf

This net triangle makes an awesome shelf for your room—it's a great place to store stuffed animals or other lightweight toys. Be sure to ask your mom or dad if it's okay to hang it, and then have them help you install the hooks to hold it up.

SKILL LEVEL

Easy

FINISHED SIZE

When stretched, about 30 inches (from the center top to the center bottom point) x 50 inches wide

MATERIALS

- 2 skeins, 172 yd/157m of medium worsted-weight yarn

- Size H (5mm) crochet hook

- Tapestry needle

- 5 to 7 wall hooks that screw into the wall

GAUGE

4 sts = 1"

STITCHES USED

Chain (ch)

Single crochet (sc)

Double crochet (dc)

Slip stitch (sl st)

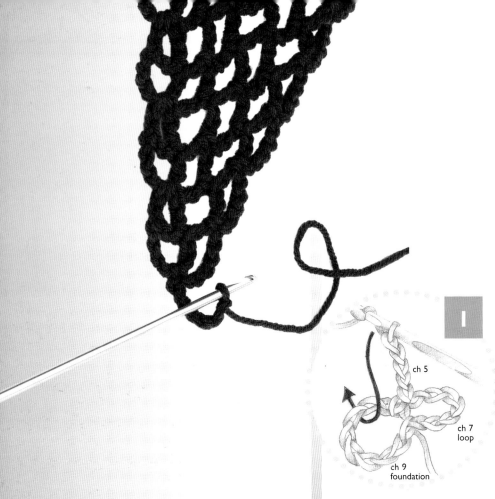

Set your shelf up in a corner of your room, as shown in figure 2. Screw the hooks into the wall about 12 inches from the ceiling, putting one in the corner (or near the corner) and the other two about 30 inches from the corner in each wall. Make sure the hooks are pointing up. Hang the corner loops of your crocheted triangle on the hooks. Fill it with stuffed animals or other lightweight toys. If you find that you toys are sagging down too much on your shelf, you can put more hooks for better support along the wall and hook the sides of the crochet work in them.

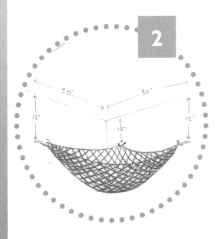

ch 5

ch 7
loop

ch 9
foundation

INSTRUCTIONS (BEGINNING AT THE CENTER BOTTOM POINT)

Foundation: Chain 9 (ch 9), slip stitch in the first stitch to join into a circle (sl st in 1st st to join into a circle), do not turn.

Row 1: Chain 7 (ch 7), single crochet in circle (sc in circle), chain 5, double crochet in circle (ch 5, dc in circle), turn. Figure 1 shows how to make the foundation and row 1.

Row 2: Chain 7 (ch 7), single crochet in the first loop, (sc in first lp), chain 5 (ch 5), single crochet in the next loop, (sc in next lp), chain 5 (ch 5), double crochet in the same loop (dc in same lp), turn.

Row 3: Chain 7 (ch 7), single crochet in the first loop (sc in first lp), chain 5, single crochet in the next loop and repeat to the end ([ch 5, sc in next lp] repeat to the end), chain 5 (ch 5), double crochet in the last loop again (dc in last lp again), turn.

Rows 4-41: Repeat row 3.

Row 42: Chain 5 (ch 5), single crochet in the first loop (sc in first lp), chain 3, single crochet in the next loop and repeat to the end ([ch 3, sc in next lp], repeat to end), chain 5 and single crochet in the last loop again (ch 5, sc in last lp again).

Weave in the end.

YARN USED

2 skeins of Coats & Clark Yarn's *Red Heart Classic*, 100% acrylic, 3 1/2 oz/100g, 172yd/157m, in Amethyst #0588

Show-Off Shawl

This shawl takes the chill off all year round. If you've made the corner shelf, you'll see that this project is just like it, but with a ruffled edge. Because it's easy to crochet, you can make several in different colors to match your moods and outfits.

SKILL LEVEL

Intermediate

FINISHED SIZE

About 33 inches (from the center top to the center bottom point) x 66 inches wide

MATERIALS

- 2 skeins, 172yd/157m each of medium worsted-weight yarn
- Size I (5.5mm) crochet hook
- Tapestry needle

GAUGE

4 sts = I"

STITCHES USED

Chain (ch)

Single crochet (sc)

Double crochet (dc)

Slip stitch (sl st)

INSTRUCTIONS

BODY OF SHAWL (BEGINNING AT THE CENTER BOTTOM POINT)

Foundation: Chain 9 (ch 9), slip stitch in the first stitch of the chain to join the chain into a circle (sl st in 1st st to join into a circle), do not turn.

Row 1: Chain 7 (ch 7), single crochet in the circle (sc in circle), chain 5 (ch 5), double crochet in the circle (dc in circle), turn.

Row 2: Chain 7 (ch 7), single crochet in the first loop (sc in first lp), chain 5 (ch 5), single crochet in the next loop (sc in next lp), chain 5 (ch 5), double crochet in the same loop (dc in same lp), turn.

Row 3: Chain 7 (ch 7), single crochet in the first loop (sc in first lp), chain 5, single crochet in the next loop and repeat to the end ([ch 5, sc in next lp] rep to the end), chain 5 (ch 5), double crochet in the last loop again (dc in last lp again), turn.

Rows 4–58: Repeat row 3. Do not turn at the end of row 58 but continue down the side with the edging.

EDGING

Row 1: Chain 3 (ch 3), 2 double crochet in the first loop (2 dc in first lp), chain 1, 2 double crochet in the next loop, repeat along one side of the shawl to the center point ([ch 1, 2 dc in next lp] rep along one side of shawl to center point), chain 1, 2 double crochet, chain 3, 2 double crochet in the loop of the center point ([ch 1, 2 dc, ch 3, 2 dc] in lp of center point), chain 1, 2 double crochet in the next loop and repeat along the second side of the shawl ([ch 1, 2 dc in next lp] rep along second

side of shawl), ending with 3 double crochet in the last loop (ending with 3 dc in last lp), turn.

Row 2: Chain 2 (ch 2), [chain 3 and double crochet] 3 times in the last loop and repeat in each chain space along the side ([ch 3, dc] 3 times in next ch sp) rep in ea ch sp along the side), then rep 6 times in the center bottom chain space (then 6 times in the center bottom ch sp), then repeat 3 times in each chain space along the next side (then rep 3 times in ea ch sp along the next side), chain 5 (ch 5), slip stitch (sl st) in the corner of the scarf.

Weave in the ends.

With an adult present, use an iron to steam press the body of the shawl, stretching it slightly to the finished measurements given above. Do not press the ruffled edge.

YARN USED

2 skeins of Reynolds Yarns' *Harmony*, 100% wool, 4oz/113gr, 172 yds/157m, in Medium Green #9.

Basic Net Bag

Make this bag small to carry shampoo and sunblock to the pool, larger for shoes and clothes, or larger still to carry your towel to the beach. Working more or less rounds will change the size. The basic instructions are for a medium-sized bag, which begins like the Key Chain. But don't stop there! Just keep crocheting around and around until you have your bag.

SKILL LEVEL

Intermediate

FINISHED SIZE

About 12 x 16 inches around

MATERIALS

- 1 skein medium worsted- or DK-weight yarn
- Size G (4mm) and I (5.5mm) crochet hooks
- Plastic or metal ring, 1/2 inch in diameter
- Stitch marker
- Tapestry needle

Optional: Two 1 1/2 to 2-inch beads, charms, or toys with a hole for stringing, needle and thread

The Basic Bag

All bags begin the same way. You begin at the bottom with single crochet stitches made around a ring, covering the ring like you did for the Key Chain on page 30. Then you make a loop of chain stitches, then a single crochet in the next stitch on the ring. When you've worked all the way around the ring, you make the single crochet stitches in the loops made from the chain stitches.

The rest of the bag is made by repeating the loops and single crochet stitches in the loops of previous rounds, spiraling around and around. You can make the bag as big or as small as you want. When the bag is finished, you make two cords using the chain stitch and thread them through one of the top rounds of the bag to make a drawstring for closing the bag.

GAUGE

4 sts = 1"

STITCHES USED

Chain (ch)

Single crochet (sc)

INSTRUCTIONS

THE BAG

Round 1 (making sts in the ring): Using the smaller hk, make a slip knot about 3 inches from the tail of the yarn. [Insert the hk in the ring, while holding the ring with your yarn hand, yo and pull through the ring, yo and pull through the two loops on the hk (you have just made a sc through the ring)] 10 times (10 sts total), sl st in the first st you made.

Round 2: [Ch 3, sc in the next sc on the ring] rep for each sc around the ring.

Round 3: Ch 4, sc in the lp made by the first ch-3 in round 2, pm in the ch-4 to mark the beginning of the rnd, [ch 4, sc in the next ch-3 lp] rep to the lp before the marker.

Round 4: Ch 5, sc in the lp with the marker, move the marker to the ch-5 lp, [ch 5, sc in the next ch-4 lp] rep to the lp before the marker.

Round 5: Ch 6, sc in the lp with the marker, move the marker to the ch-6 lp, [ch 6, sc in the next ch-5 lp] rep to the lp before the marker.

Round 6 (Increase rnd): Ch 6, sc in the lp with the marker, move the marker to the ch-6 lp. Ch 6, sc in the same lp again, [ch 6, sc in the next lp, ch 6, sc in the same lp] rep to the lp before the marker. You now have twice as many lps around, and continue by working into each lp.

Round 7: Ch 6, sc in the lp with the marker. Move the marker to the ch-6 lp you just made, [ch 6, sc in the next ch-6 lp] rep to the lp before the marker.

Rep round 7, until the bag is as long as you want. Weave in ends.

THE DRAWSTRING

1. Holding two strands of yarn tog as one, and using the larger hk, make a slip knot about 3 inches from the tail and make a ch long enough to go around the top of the bag when open, plus about 10 inches. Cut the yarn about 3 inches from the last lp and pull through to end the cord. Rep to make another cord. Weave in the ends.

2. Weave one cord in and out along one of the top rounds of the bag until you have gone all the way around. Beg weaving the other cord at the opposite side of the bag, weaving through the same holes so the ends of the new cord end up on the opposite side. Tie the ends of each cord tog in a knot.

Optional: A bead, charm, or toy that's sewed to the cord where it's attached to the bag will help you pull the bag open. To do this, work all the instructions for the basic bag then make the drawstring as above, but make it 15 inches longer than the bag opening. Fold one cord of the drawstring in half and tie it around one loop of the bag along the round you will be weaving through. Weave both ends through the round to the opposite side. Tie the other cord in the same way where the first cord ends. Hold the two ends of one cord together and tie them into a knot. Sew a toy, charm, or bead to the part of the cord that is tied to the bag.

YARN USED

1 skein of Lorna's Laces Yarns' *Shepherd*, 100% worsted-weight yarn, 4oz/115g, 225yd/206m, in Rainbow

Really, Really Big Bag!

This bag is just like the basic net bag, except it's BIG! You can use it for storage—just hang it on a hook in your closet and fill it with anything from sports equipment to favorite toys. Or use it for getting everything you need to the game. It's also great for carrying your overnight essentials to a sleepover.

SKILL LEVEL

Intermediate

FINISHED SIZE

About 17 x 48 inches around

MATERIALS

- 2 skeins of medium worsted-weight yarn

- Sizes H (5mm) and J (6mm) crochet hooks

- Plastic or metal ring

- Stitch marker

- Tapestry needle

GAUGE

4 sts = 1"

STITCHES USED

Chain (ch)

Single crochet (sc)

Slip stitch (sl st)

INSTRUCTIONS

THE BAG

Round 1: (Making the sts in the ring): Using the smaller size hk, make a slip knot about 3 inches from the tail of the yarn. [Insert the hk in the ring, while holding the ring with your yarn hand, yo and pull through the ring, yo and pull through the two loops on the hk (you have just made a sc through the ring)] 10 times (10 sts total), sl st in the first st you made.

Round 2: [Ch 3, sc in the next sc on the ring] rep in each sc around the ring.

Round 3: Ch 4, sc in the lp made from the first ch-3 in round 2, pm in the ch-4 to mark the beginning of the rnd, [ch 4, sc in the next ch-3 lp] rep to the lp before the marker.

Round 4: Ch 5, sc in the lp with the marker, move the marker to the ch-5 lp, [ch 5, sc in the next ch-4 lp] rep to the lp before the marker.

Round 5: Ch 6, sc in the lp with the marker, move the marker to the ch-6 lp, [ch 6, sc in the next ch-5 lp] rep to the lp before the marker.

Round 6 (Increase rnd): Ch 6, sc in the lp with the marker, move the marker to the ch-6 lp. Ch 6, sc in the same lp again, [ch 6, sc in the next lp, ch 6, sc in the same lp] rep to the lp before the marker. You now have twice as many lps around. Continue by working into each lp.

Round 7: Ch 6, sc in the lp with the marker. Move the marker to the ch-6 lp you just made, [ch 6, sc in the next ch-6 lp] rep to the lp before the marker.

Round 8 (Increase rnd): Ch 6, sc in the lp with the marker, move the marker to the ch-6 lp you just made. Ch 6, sc in the same lp again, [ch 6, sc in the next lp, ch 6, sc in the same lp] rep to the lp before the marker. You now have twice as many lps around, and continue by working into each lp.

Rep round 7, until the bag is as long as you want. Weave in the ends.

THE DRAWSTRING

1. Holding two strands of yarn tog as one, and using the larger hk, make a slip knot about 3 inches from the tail and make a ch long enough to go around the top of the bag when open, plus about 10 inches. Cut the yarn about 3 inches from the last lp and pull through to end the cord. Rep to make another cord. Weave in the ends.

2. Weave one cord in and out along one of the top rounds of the bag until you have gone all the way around. Beg weaving the other cord at the opposite side of the bag, weaving through the same holes so the new ends of the cord are on the opposite side. Tie the ends of the cords tog in a knot.

YARN USED

2 skeins Caron Yarns' *Wintuk*, 100% acrylic, 3 1/2oz/99g, 150yd/135m, in Christmas Red #3005

Small Lace-Edged Bag

Here's another way to change the look of the basic bag. By using thinner cotton yarn and adding a ruffle, you can create a more delicate design for a dressed-up look.

SKILL LEVEL

Advanced Intermediate

FINISHED SIZE

About 8 inches x 9 inches around

MATERIALS

- 1 skein, lightweight sport-weight yarn
- Sizes F (3.75mm) and H (5mm) crochet hooks
- Plastic or metal ring
- Stitch marker
- Tapestry needle

Optional: Two ½-inch charms, needle, and thread

GAUGE

4 sts = 1"

STITCHES USED

Chain (ch)

Single crochet (sc)

Slip stitch (sl st)

INSTRUCTIONS

THE BAG

Round 1 (Making the sts in the ring): Using the smaller size hk, make a slip knot about 3 inches from the tail of the yarn. [Insert the hk in the ring, while holding the ring with your yarn hand, yo and pull through the ring, yo and pull through the two loops on the hk (you have just made a sc through the ring)] 10 times (10 sts total), sl st in the first st you made.

Round 2: [Ch 3, sc in the next sc on the ring] rep in each sc around the ring.

Round 3: Ch 4, sc in the lp made from the first ch-3 in round 2, pm in the ch-4 to mark the beginning of the rnd, [ch 4, sc in the next ch-3 lp] rep to the lp before the marker.

Round 4: Ch 5, sc in the lp with the marker, move the marker to the ch-5 lp, [ch 5, sc in the next ch-4 lp] rep to the lp before the marker.

Round 5: Ch 6, sc in the lp with the marker, move the marker to the ch-6 lp, [ch 6, sc in the next ch-5 lp] rep to the lp before the marker.

Rep round 5, until the bag is as long as you want.

For the last round, ch 3, make 3 sc in the lp with the marker. Move the marker to the ch-3 loop. Ch 3, make 3 sc in the same lp.

[Ch 3, make 3 sc in the next lp, ch 3, make 3 sc in the same lop] Rep to the lp before the marker. Weave in the ends.

THE DRAWSTRING

1. Holding two strands of yarn tog as one, and using the larger hk, make a slip knot about 3 inches from the tail and make a ch long enough to go around the top of the bag when open, plus about 15 inches. Cut the yarn about 3 inches from the last lp and pull through to end the cord. Rep to make another cord. Weave in the ends.

2. Fold one cord of the drawstring in half and tie it around one loop of the bag along the round you will be weaving through, about 3 or 4 rounds down from the top. Weave both ends through the round to the opposite side. Tie the other cord in the same way where the first cord ends. Hold the two ends of one cord together and tie them into a knot. Optional: sew a toy, charm, or bead to part of the cord that is tied to the bag.

YARN USED

1 skein of Dale of Norway Yarn's *Svale* 50% cotton/10% silk/40% viscose, 1^3/$_4$oz/50g, 114yd/105m, in Pale Yellow #2005.

CHALLENGE YOURSELF!

Ready to challenge your skills? You can do it! Because these projects have more instructions to follow, they'll take longer to complete. In fact, you might find it helpful to make an appointment with your crocheting—several times a week; set aside the same 20 to 30 minutes for your crochet work.

Chemistry Pillows

These are called "chemistry" pillows because making them is like doing a chemistry experiment—you try things out to see what will happen. You can start out with one design idea, and then change it as you go—mix yarns, try different stitch combinations—there are no rules, and if you make a mistake, nothing will blow up!

SKILL LEVEL

Intermediate

■ BLUE PILLOW

FINISHED SIZE

18 x 18 inches

MATERIALS

- 2 skeins of bulky weight yarn, each in a different color
- Size K (6.5–7mm) crochet hook
- 18-inch-square pillow form
- Stitch marker
- Tapestry needle

GAUGE

9 sts = 4"

5 rows = 4"

STITCHES USED

Chain (ch)

Single crochet (sc)

Double crochet (dc)

INSTRUCTIONS

Foundation: Ch 35, turn.

Round 1: Ch 1, sc in the back half of the second ch and ea ch to the last ch, 5 sc in the last ch, sc in the other half of ea ch to the first ch, 4 sc in the first ch, pm.

Round 2: Ch 3, dc in ea st around, join to top of ch 3, do not turn.

Rep round 2, changing colors as you want to, until your crocheting measures 18 inches from round 1. (The sample was made of 7 rounds of blue, 1 round of chenille, 1 round of blue, 2 rounds of chenille, 2 rounds of chenille, 1 round of blue, 3 rounds of chenille, and 4 rounds of blue).

Cut the yarn to about 24 inches and pull the tail through the last loop.

ASSEMBLY

Slide the pillow form inside the crochet work. Thread the 24-inch tail on a tapestry needle and sew the opening together. Weave in any loose ends.

■ RIBBON PILLOW

This pillow uses different patterns and stitches. It's begun in the same way as the basic pillow on page 84.

FINISHED SIZE

16 x 16 inches

MATERIALS

- 6 skeins of lightweight sport-weight yarn
- Size H (5 mm) crochet hook

- Tapestry needle
- Stitch marker
- 16-inch pillow form

Optional: 2 yards of ³/₈-inch-wide ribbon, matching colored thread, and a sewing needle

GAUGE

4 sc sts = 1"

STITCHES USED

Chain (ch)

Single crochet (sc)

Double crochet (dc)

INSTRUCTIONS

Use two strands of yarn held together as one throughout.

Foundation: Make a slip knot about 3 inches from the end of the yarn, and ch 55, turn.

Round 1: Ch 1, sc in back half of 2nd ch from hk and the back half of ea st across to the last st, 5 sc in the last st, sc in the other half of each st across to the first st, 4 sc in half of the first st (116 sts total), pm, do not turn.

Rounds 2-6: Sc in ea st around.

Round 7: Sc in the back half of ea st.

Round 8: Dc in ea st around.

Round 9: [Ch 1, sk 1 st, dc in the next st] rep around.

Round 10: Dc in ea st and ch around.

Round 11: Sc in ea st around.

Round 12: Sc in the back half of ea st around.

Rounds 13-15: Sc in ea st around.

Rounds 16-18: Dc in ea st around.

Round 19: Sc in ea st around.

Rounds 20-25: Rep rows 7-12.

Rounds 26-28: Dc in ea st around.

Rounds 29-32: Sc in ea st around.

Rounds 33-38: Rep rows 7-12.

Rounds 39-43: Sc in ea st around.

End with a 24-inch tail.

ASSEMBLY

If you want to add the ribbon, thread the tapestry needle with the ribbon, and weave it in and out of the double crochet along row 9. Bring both ends of the ribbon to the inside of the pillow. Slide the pillow form inside before cutting the ribbon to be sure the ribbon isn't pulled too tight, then take the pillow form out. Cut the ribbon so there is about ¹/₂ inch extra inside the pillow. Sew these ends together with the sewing needle and thread. Repeat for the other two rows with open spaces between the stitches. Insert the pillow form into the crochet work. Thread the tapestry needle with the 24-inch tail and sew the opening shut. Weave in the ends.

YARNS USED

BLUE PILLOW

1 skein of Lion Brand Yarns' *Homespun*, 98% acrylic/2% polyester, 6oz/170g, 185yd/169m, in Barrington #336

1 skein Lion Brand Yarns' chenille *Thick and Quick*, 91% acrylic/9% polyester, 4oz/112g, 100yd/91m, in Periwinkle #107

RIBBON PILLOW

6 skeins of Paton's Yarns' *Kroy Socks*, 75% washable wool/25% nylon, 1³/₄oz/50g, 192yd/175m, in Winter Eclipse #54561

The Basic Pillow

These pillow projects are worked in the round, beginning with a chain foundation. You single crochet in the back half of each stitch, then make 5 single crochet in the last stitch. Then you continue around to the other side of the chain, and single crochet in the other half of all the chain stitches. You'll see that you've made a big elongated oval. Finally, you make 4 single crochet in the back half of the first chain, to complete the round. Now you begin working in a big spiral, making your stitches in all the stitches around and around.

Pocket Scarf & Matching Hat

Don't be caught out in the cold, be cool while keeping warm! The extra-long hat and matching scarf with hand-warming pockets are made with a large hook and thick yarn so you can make this set in a weekend.

SKILL LEVEL

Intermediate

FINISHED SIZES

HAT

33 inches long, including tassel (to fit head sizes 20 to 23 inches around)

SCARF

8 x 56 inches

STITCHES USED

Chain (ch)

Single crochet (sc)

Half double crochet (hdc)

MATERIALS

SCARF

- 3 skeins of variegated-color bulky weight yarn

- Size N (9mm) crochet hook

- Large tapestry needle

HAT

- 3 skeins of bulky weight yarn, 1 in blue and 2 variegated

- Size N (9mm) crochet hook

- Large tapestry needle

- Stitch marker

GAUGE

7 sts = 4"

4 rows = 4"

INSTRUCTIONS

■ SCARF

Foundation: Ch 12, turn.

Row 1: Ch 2, hdc in 3rd ch from hk and ea ch across, turn (12 sts total).

Rows 2–83: Ch 2, hdc in ea st across, turn.

To make the pockets

1. Fold the end of the scarf up at the 9th row from the last row you made.

2. Insert the hook through the end of the last row you made and into the end of the 18th row from the end of the scarf (if you folded the end up at the 9th row, the 18th row will be right next to the hook at the end of the scarf). See figure 1.

3. Make a sc through the last st of both the 9th and 18th rows along the side edge of the scarf.

4. Continuing along the side edge of the scarf, and working toward the bottom corner of the pocket, make 2 sc in the end of each row, working through both thicknesses where the pocket is forming.

5. At the corner, make 3 sc in the last st.

6. Make 1 sc in ea st along the bottom of the pocket (this is the 9th row where you folded the scarf up in step 1).

7. Make 3 sc in the other corner at the bottom of the pocket, then make 2 sc in the end of each row working through both thicknesses up the other side of the pocket, and then through the single thickness of the scarf along one side until 18 rows from the other end of the scarf.

8. Fold up the other end of the scarf along the 9th row from the end and continue with 2 sc in the end of ea row, working through two thicknesses along the pocket sides, 3 sc in the corners, and 1 sc in ea st along the bottom of the pocket.

9. Continue with 2 sc in the end of ea row along the edge of the scarf until you reach your starting point of the first pocket. Weave in the ends.

■ HAT

Using the solid-color yarn, begin at the seam of the cuff and work sideways.

Foundation: Ch 10, turn.

Row 1: Ch 1, sc in 2nd ch from hk and ea ch across, turn (10 sts total).

Row 2: Ch 1, sc in ea st across, turn.

Repeat row 2 until the crochet is about 20 to 21 inches long, or until it fits around your head, when you stretch it slightly. Sew the side seam of the cuff so the crochet work is in a tube shape. Weave in the end.

Body of the Hat

Round 1: Attach the variegated yarn to the seam, and sc in the end of ea row along one long edge of the brim, as shown in figure 2. Place marker.

Rounds 2–5: Hdc in ea st around.

Round 6: Sk 1st st (one dec), hdc in ea st around.

Repeat round 6 until there are only 4 sts left. Cut the yarn, leaving a 12-inch tail for attaching the tassel.

sc in end of each row

2

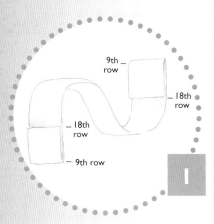

9th row

18th row

18th row

9th row

1

MAKING THE TASSEL

To make the tassel, cut six 18-inch lengths of ea color of yarn. Holding the 12 strands of yarn as one, fold them in half and make a knot close to the folded end. Don't tighten the knot all the way. Thread the tapestry needle with the 12-inch tail on the hat and pass the needle through the fold in the tassel, as shown in figure 3. Now tighten the tassel knot as close to the fold as possible. Sew the tassel to the end of the hat and weave in the end of the yarn. Trim the ends of the tassel so they are all the same length.

YARN USED

6 skeins Paton's Yarns' *Melody Quick and Cozy*, 100% acrylic, 85yds/78m, 3¹/₂oz/100g.

HAT:

1 skein of Peacock #09742 and 2 skeins of Fun 'n Games #09741

SCARF:

3 skeins of Fun 'n Games #09741

3

Top
of Hat

Zippy Summer Top

When it's hot outside and you want to look great, make this beautiful lacy top. It's way cool! All you do is crochet a rectangle, connect it in the middle with a zipper, and you're ready to go.

SKILL LEVEL

Advanced Intermediate

FINISHED SIZE

Width: Your chest measurement minus 1½ inches (to make it stretch to fit)

Length: 11½ inches, not including the straps

MATERIALS

- 2 skeins of medium worsted-weight cotton or cotton blend in a cream-colored yarn
- Size G (4mm) crochet hook
- 10-inch separating zipper
- Sewing needle and thread to match yarn color
- Tapestry needle
- Safety pins
- Straight pins

GAUGE IN DOUBLE CROCHET

18 sts = 4"

9 rows = 4"

STITCHES USED

Chain (ch)

Single crochet (sc)

Double crochet (dc)

Slip stitch (sl st)

INSTRUCTIONS

BODY

Foundation: Ch 44, turn.

Row 1: Ch 3, dc in 4th ch from hk and ea ch across, turn (44 sts total).

Row 2: Ch 3, dc in ea st across, turn.

Stop here and hold the small strip up to you to see if it is going to be too long or too short. It's sort of hard to visualize it at this point, but try. Remember that you will be adding a bottom edging that is about 1-inch wide. If you need to change the length, start again with more or less stitches to get the length you want.

Repeat row 2 until the crochet work is equal to your chest measurement minus 1 1/2 inches.

Stop here and hold the crochet work around you to see if it is too small or too large. Keep in mind the zipper section will be about 1/2-inch wide. You want the bodice to stretch a little to fit, but not be too tight. You may need to take out or add a few rows to get the correct fit.

Continuing with the same yarn and working along the bottom edge, (ch 5, sl st in the 3rd ch from hk, ch 2, sc in the next ch-3 along the edge) repeat along one long side edge of the rectangle, ending at the corner. Weave in the ends.

Sew the beg row and end row to the sides of the zipper.

SHOULDER STRAPS

Make two. Try on the top and have someone use a measuring tape to see how long the shoulder straps should be. Put safety pins where you want the shoulder straps to attach at the front and back. Multiply the length of your strap in inches times 5.

Ch that number, turn.

Ch 1, sc in the back half of the 2nd ch from the hk and the back half of ea ch across.

Continuing around the end of the strip, ch 4, sl st in the 3rd ch from the hk, ch 1, sc in the end of the strip, (ch 4, sl st in the 3rd ch from the hk, ch 1, sk 2, sc in the next st) repeat along one side of the strip, the other end of the strip, and the remaining back half of the strip. Set aside.

ASSEMBLY

Pin the straps to the top where it is marked with the safety pins, overlapping the straps about 1 inch on the front and back of the blouse.

Stop here and try on the blouse, and adjust the placement of the straps, if needed, for proper fit. Then, using the sewing thread and needle, sew the straps to the top.

YARN USED

2 skeins of Brown Sheep Company Inc. Yarns', *Cotton Fleece*, 80% cotton/20% merino wool, 3 1/2 oz/100g, 215yd/197m, in Putty #CW-105.

Getting It to Fit

Making clothes to fit your body is a little different than making a hat or a scarf. You almost always have to adjust the pattern a little to your own measurements so the garment will fit you properly. The best way to check if a pattern is the right size for you is to measure a similar piece of clothing that you already have—in this case, a close-fitting tank top. By doing this, you'll have some idea of how big to make the crocheted piece.

This top is meant to be close fitting, so it will actually be the same measurement as your chest or a little smaller. You should try it on at different stages as you crochet so you can see if the top is too loose or too tight, and to measure where to place the straps and how long you want them to be. A good fit is just as important as a good design in determining how a finished crochet piece will look.

CD Case

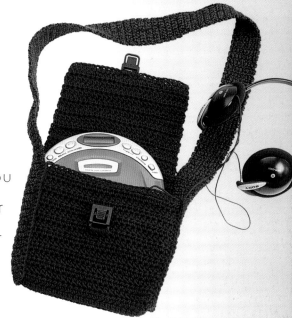

By crocheting two long rectangles, you can make this case for carrying your portable CD player, or your music, or game CDs. It's an easy project, but takes a little more time since you're using a smaller hook and yarn. Sewing a purchased buckle on the flap is an easy way to finish the bag, and will hold everything securely inside.

SKILL LEVEL

Intermediate

FINISHED SIZE

6 x 5 1/2 x 1 1/2 inches, with a 24-inch-long strap

MATERIALS

- 1 skein each of fine sport-weight cotton yarn in purple and magenta
- Sizes C (2.75mm) and E (3.5mm) crochet hooks
- Small black plastic two-part buckle
- Tapestry needle
- Needle and thread

GAUGE

With C hook in single crochet

24 sts = 4"

25 rows = 4"

With E hook in half double crochet

18 sts = 4"

13 rows = 4"

STITCHES USED

Chain (ch)

Single crochet (sc)

Half double crochet (hdc)

INSTRUCTIONS

THE CASE

Foundation: Using the E hook and purple yarn, ch 25, turn.

Row 1: Ch 2, hdc in 3rd ch from the hk and ea ch across, turn.

Rows 2–52: Ch 2, hdc in ea st across, turn.

Weave in the ends.

THE STRAP

Foundation: Using the C hook and magenta yarn, ch 8, turn.

Row 1: Ch 1, sc in 2nd ch from hk and ea ch across, turn.

Rows 2–224: Ch 1, sc in ea st across, turn.

Weave in the ends.

ASSEMBLY

Find the 28th row from one end of the strap, and place it by the first row of the case. Hold both pieces together, and use the C hook and purple yarn to sc through the edge of both pieces. Work around the case as shown in figure 1 until you come to row 36 of the strap. Weave in the ends. Repeat for the other end of the strap and opposite side of the case.

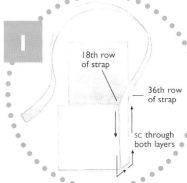

18th row of strap

36th row of strap

sc through both layers

Sew the top half of the purchased buckle to the center of the top flap's edge, and the bottom half to the front of the bag. You want the top and bottom of the buckle to line up when the flap is closed. It will help to fill the case with CDs, and then mark where the bottom half of the buckle will go before sewing it.

YARN USED

1 skein of Tahki Imports Ltd. Yarns' *Cotton Classic*, 100% mercerized cotton, 1¾oz/50g, 108yd/100m, in color #429 (magenta)

1 skein of Mouzakis Yarns' *Butterfly*, DK yarn, 100% mercerized cotton, 1¾oz/50g, 108yd/100m, in color #3928 (purple)

The buckle is by La Mode #4801, ½ inch (12mm) in Black

Felted Backpack

f you find your old backpack is getting stuffed with stuff, grab your crochet hook and make a new one! Because you shrink this one to felt it, be sure to make it large enough to begin with so it can hold all your essentials. If you want to change the finished size to make a bigger or smaller backpack, make more or less of the increase rounds when you crochet the bottom section.

SKILL LEVEL

Advanced Intermediate

FINISHED SIZE

Before felting: 19 x 18 inches, not including the flap

After felting: About 15 x 15 inches, not including the flap

MATERIALS

- 3 skeins of medium worsted-weight wool yarn in light brown

- 1 skein each of medium worsted-weight wool yarn in dark brown, black, and cream

- Size I (5.5mm) crochet hook

- Tapestry needle

- Stitch marker

- 54-inch shoelace

- White cotton crochet cord to baste top closed for felting

- Mesh laundry bag

- Washer and dryer

GAUGE BEFORE FELTING

14 sts = 4"

15 rows = 4"

STITCHES USED

Chain (ch)

Single crochet (sc)

INSTRUCTIONS

THE PACK

Foundation: Using the light brown yarn, ch 2, turn.

Round 1: 6 sc in the second ch from hk, do not turn.

Round 2: 2 sc in ea st around, pm (12 sts total).

Round 3: (Sc in next st, 2 sc in next st) 6 times, pm (18 sts total).

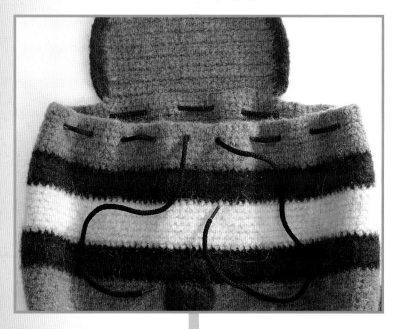

Round 4: (Sc in next 2 sts, 2 sc in next st) 6 times, pm (24 sts total).

Round 5: (Sc in next 3 sts, 2 sc in next st) 6 times, pm (30 sts total).

Round 6: (Sc in next 4 sts, 2 sc in next st) 6 times, pm (36 sts total).

Round 7: (Sc in next 5 sts, 2 sc in next st) 6 times, pm (42 sts total).

Round 8: (Sc in next 6 sts, 2 sc in next st) 6 times, pm (48 sts total).

Continue in this pattern, working one more sc in ea repeat before the 2 sc, until you work one round with 19 sc, then 2 sc in ea rep (126 sts total).

Work even with 1 sc in ea st for 18 rounds.

Change to black yarn, work 1 round.

Change to dark brown yarn, work 3 rounds.

Change to black yarn, work 1 round.

Change to cream yarn, work 7 rounds.

Change to black yarn, work 1 round.

Change to dark brown yarn, work 3 rounds.

Change to black yarn, work 1 round.

Change to light brown yarn, work 7 rounds.

Remove the marker.

THE FLAP

Continuing with the light brown yarn, sc in the next 15 sts, turn.

Row 1: Ch 1, sc in next 30 sts, turn.

Rows 2–10: Ch 1, sc in ea st across, turn.

Rows 11–36: Ch 1, sk next st, sc in ea st across, turn (1 st decreased ea row, 4 sts remaining after row 36).

Rows 37–40: Ch 1, sc in ea st across, turn.

Rows 41–46: Ch 1, sc in ea st across, sc in ch 1 at end of row turn, (1 st increased ea row, 10 sts total after row 46).

Rows 47–50: Ch 1, sc in ea st across, turn.

Rows 51–57: Ch 1, sk next st, sc in ea st across, turn (1 st decreased ea row, 3 sts remaining after row 57).

Weave in the ends.

Dark Brown Edging on the Flap

Attach the dark brown yarn to one edge of row 34.

Sc along the side of the flap to the backpack, turn.

Ch 1, sc in ea sc of the dark brown yarn. Weave in the ends.

Repeat on the other side of the flap.

Loop for Closing Flap

Foundation: Using the dark brown yarn, begin with an 8-inch tail to use for attaching the loop to the backpack, ch 4, turn.

Row 1: Ch 1, sc in 2nd ch from hk and ea ch across, turn (4 sts).

Rows 2–10: Ch 1, sc in ea st across, turn.

Cut the yarn 8 inches from the crochet work and pull the tail through the last st.

Fold the backpack in half to find the center front. Using the 8-inch tails and the tapestry needle, sew the loop to the backpack attaching it 3 sts on either side of the front, just below the bottom black stripe. Weave in the ends.

STRAPS

Make two.

Foundation: Using the dark brown yarn, begin with a 12-inch tail to use for attaching the strap to the backpack, ch 7, turn.

Row 1: Ch 1, sc in 2nd ch from hk and ea ch across, turn (7 sts).

Rows 2–70: Ch 1, sc in ea st across, turn.

Cut the yarn 12 inches from the crochet work, and pull the tail through the last st.

ASSEMBLY

Using the tapestry needle and the 12-inch tails attached to the straps, sew one end of ea strap to the center back of the backpack, just above the top row of black. Sew the other end of the straps 6 inches up from the center bottom, and 3 1/2 inches from the center back of the backpack.

FELTING

Take the shoelace and weave it in and out of the backpack stitches, two rows down from the top edge, passing over 6 sts then under 6 sts, and beginning and ending at the center front. Tie the ends into a loose knot. Use the cotton cord to baste the flap to the backpack opening, leaving the pull-through tab hanging loose. You will take the basting stitches out after felting. Put your crochet work in the mesh laundry bag. Now throw it in your washer set to the lowest water level and to the hot wash and cold rinse setting. Don't put it in the washer with towels, because the lint from the towels can shed and get into the fibers of your felted bag. Put about 1 tablespoon of liquid dish soap in the washer. Check several times during the wash cycle to see if it's felted. Wash it again if nothing has happened. If you want it to shrink it some more after it's been washed, put it in the dryer. Or, if it shrunk enough, you can let it dry in a warm, dry place.

YARN USED

6 skeins of Brown Sheep Company, Inc. Yarns' *Lamb's Pride* worsted-weight yarn, 85% wool/15% mohair, 4 oz/113 g, 190 yd/173 m, 3 skeins in Oak #8, 1 skein each in Coffee #89, Onyx #5, and Cream #10.

SHINE & DAZZLE

an't afford more sparkle in your life because your
allowance is maxed out? Make your own accessories.
A beaded barrette, amulet bag, fancy edging for a
shirt, bookmark, and a necklace, will let you shine
even if it's weeks—or just seems like it—to your next
allowance. Most of these projects are easy, but because they
use smaller hooks and crochet cord instead of thick
yarn, they're meant for intermediate crocheters.

Beaded Barrette

ou're sure to get attention when these beads glisten in your hair. You'll want several for yourself—but they also make great gifts for friends. You string the beads on the cord before you begin to crochet, then move the beads up as you work to create the dangling loops.

SKILL LEVEL

Intermediate

FINISHED SIZE

About 2 x 3 inches

MATERIALS

- 1 ball of dark blue crochet cotton, size 3

- Size B (2.25mm) crochet hook

- 234 beads that are large enough to string onto the yarn (size 5 or 6 seed beads)

- Size 10 beading needle

- About a 10-inch length of beading thread

- Tapestry needle

- Craft glue

- 3-inch wide barrette

GAUGE

24 sts = 4"

22 rows = 4"

STITCHES USED

Chain (ch)

Single crochet (sc)

INSTRUCTIONS

PREPARATION

Tie the beading thread to the crochet cotton, then thread the beading needle with the beading thread. This allows you to string the beads onto the crochet cotton using the thin needle. String 234 beads onto the crochet cotton. For this barrette, two colors of blue beads were mixed and then strung randomly. When you're done, slide the thread off the crochet cotton.

Foundation: Ch 20, turn.

Row 1: Ch 1, sc in the ch-2 from hk and ea ch across, turn (20 sts total).

Row 2: Ch 1, sc in ea st across, turn.

Row 3: As shown in figure 1, [slide 5 beads up to the crochet work, sc in the next st, so the beads form a loop]

rep for ea st across, increasing 2 beads ea st (7, 9, 11, 13, etc.), until you have 21 beads in the loop. Make one more with 21, then start decreasing until on the last st of the row you are back to 5 beads in the loop. Weave in the ends.

ASSEMBLY

Glue the crocheted strip to the barrette with the beads hanging below the barrette.

YARN USED

1 ball of Coats & Clark Yarns' *J. P. Coats Royal Fashion Crochet Thread*, size 3, 100% mercerized cotton, 150yd/137m, in Navy #0486.

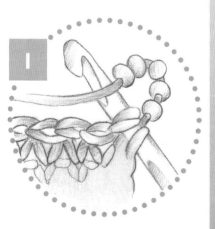

Amulet Bag

This little amulet bag features a beaded heart made by simply sliding beads into the crochet work at different times. Sometimes patterns like this use charts to show you where to put the beads, but this pattern gives you line-by-line directions like the other projects in this book. As you work you may notice that what you normally think of as the backside of the crochet has become the front because of the way you work in the beads. This is perfectly okay, and is the way it's done for this type of project.

SKILL LEVEL

Intermediate

FINISHED SIZE

About 2 x 2 inches, with a 20-inch strap

MATERIALS

- 1 ball of red crochet cotton cord, size 3
- Size B (2.25mm) crochet hook
- Tapestry needle
- Stitch marker

- 46 beads large enough to string onto the cord
- Size 10 beading needle
- About a 10-inch length of beading thread

GAUGE

26 sts = 4"

28 rows = 4"

STITCHES USED

Chain (ch)

Single crochet (sc)

Slip stitch (sl st)

INSTRUCTIONS

PREPARATION

Tie the thread to the crochet cotton and thread it on the beading needle. This allows you to string the beads onto the cotton using the thin needle. Pick up the beads with the needle and slide them down the thread and onto the cord until you have all 46 beads on the cord. Slide the knotted thread off the cord.

SPECIAL ABBREVIATION

You'll notice that these instructions have a new abbreviation, bc, for bead crochet. This tells you which stitches will have the beads. You read it this way: 3 bc means that you make three single crochet stitches, each using one bead. When it's time to use a bead you just slide it into position. Figure 1 shows you how to work the bead into the stitch.

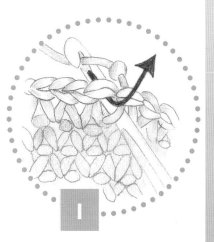

1

Foundation: Begin with a 12-inch tail (you'll use this later to stitch the bottom of the bag together), ch 28, sl st into the first ch to join the chain into a circle, pm, do not turn.

Round 1: Ch 1, sc in ea ch around.

Round 2: Sc in ea st around.

Rounds 3–4: 6 sc, 1 bc, 21 sc.

Round 5: 5 sc, 3 bc, 20 sc.

Round 6: 4 sc, 5 bc, 19 sc.

Rounds 7–8: 3 sc, 7 bc, 18 sc.

Round 9: 3 sc, 3 bc, 1 sc, 3 bc, 18 sc.

Round 10: 4 sc, 1 bc, 3 sc, 1 bc, 19 sc.

Rounds 11–12: Sc in ea st around.

Round 13: [1 sc, 1 bc] repeat around.

Round 14: Sc in ea st around.

STRAP

Continuing with the working cord, ch 110, sl st in the opposite side of the top of the bag, sl st one st away along the top of the bag, turn, sc in the back loop of ea ch back to the other side of the bag. Weave in the end. Stitch the bottom of the bag together using the 12-inch tail.

BLOCKING

The finished bag will slant slightly. To correct this you need to block the bag. Wet the bag in cool water and pull it to shape, so the stitches line up vertically. Place the bag on a towel and let it dry in a warm place overnight.

YARNS USED

1 ball of Coats & Clark Yarns' *J. P. Coats Royal Fashion Crochet Thread*, size 3, 100% mercerized cotton, 150yd/137m, in Scarlet #0006.

Corner Bookmark

n the 1920s through the 1950s, it was popular for ladies to crochet delicate doilies for decorating their tables. They used small hooks and thin crochet cord to make the lacy patterns. This design will give you good practice working crochet in a similar way. But instead of a doily, you'll make a much more useful corner bookmark with bead dangles to hold your place in your favorite book.

SKILL LEVEL

Advanced Intermediate

FINISHED SIZE

About 3 x 3 inches

MATERIALS

- 1 ball green crochet cotton cord in size 3
- Size B (2.25mm) crochet hook
- Tapestry needle
- Spray starch
- Iron
- About 10 beads, each large enough to slide onto the cotton cord
- Thick white craft glue

GAUGE

26 sts = 4"

28 rows = 4"

STITCHES USED

Chain (ch)

Single crochet (sc)

Double crochet (dc)

INSTRUCTIONS

FAN SHAPE

Foundation: Leaving a 3 to 4-inch tail, ch 4, turn.

Row 1: 4 dc in 4th ch from hk, turn.

Row 2: Ch 3, dc in 1st st, ch 1, sk 1 st, [2 dc, ch 1, 2 dc] in next st, ch 1, sk 1 st, 2 dc in top of ch 4, turn.

Row 3: Ch 3, dc in 1st st, ch 1, dc in ch sp, ch 1, [2 dc, ch 1, 2 dc] in next ch sp, ch 1, dc in ch sp, ch 1, 2 dc in top of ch 4, turn.

Row 4: Ch 3, dc in 1st st, [ch 1, dc in ch sp] twice, ch 1, [2 dc, ch 1, 2 dc] in next ch sp, [ch 1, dc in ch sp] twice, ch 1, 2 dc in top of ch 4, turn.

Row 5: Ch 3, dc in 1st st, [ch 1, dc in ch sp] 3 times, ch 1, [2 dc, ch 1, 2 dc] in next ch sp, [ch 1, dc in ch sp] 3 times, ch 1, 2 dc in top of ch 4, turn.

Row 6: Ch 3, dc in 1st st, [ch 1, dc in ch sp] 4 times, ch 1, [2 dc, ch 1, 2 dc] in next ch sp, [ch 1, dc in ch sp] 4 times, ch 1, 2 dc in top of ch 4, turn.

Row 7: Ch 4, sc in ch sp, [ch 4, sk next ch sp, sc in next ch sp] 2 times, ch 4, sc in next ch sp, ch 1, sc in same ch sp, ch 4, sc in next ch sp [ch 4, sk next ch sp, sc in next ch sp] 2 times, ch 4, sc in top of ch 4.

Weave in the working end, but not the tail you left at the beginning. Make another fan shape following the directions above, except don't cut the yarn or weave in the end after Row 7.

ASSEMBLY

Hold the two fan shapes together with the last one you made on the top. Attach the sides together by making all the sc in the following directions through both fan shapes held together as one.

Sc in corner of both fan shapes held tog as one.

Ch 4, sc in end of row 7, [ch 4, sc in end of next row along side] rep for ea row. At corner, [ch 4, sc in corner] twice, then ch 4, sc in row 1, [ch 4, sc in next row] rep for ea row along the other side. Weave in the end.

String the beads onto the tails as shown in the photo. Tie a knot at the end of ea tail to hold the beads in place. Put a dot of glue on the tail to lock it in place. Let the glue dry, and then spray the finished bookmark with spray starch and use the iron to steam press it until it's flat and stiff.

YARN USED

1 ball of Coats & Clark Yarn's J. P. *Coats Royal Fashion Crochet Thread*, size 3, 100% mercerized cotton, 150yd/137m, in Lime #0264.

Shirt Edging

Love your t-shirts, but feel like they're missing something? Add some color and texture with crochet edgings. The shirts used here already had small looped trim along the edge, making it easy to crochet into. If your shirt doesn't have this, you could add the loops using a needle and thread or the crochet cotton. If the knit is loose enough, you could even crochet right into the edge of the shirt. This pattern gives you two edgings—one uses a single crochet, and the other uses picot to make it more decorative.

SKILL LEVEL

Intermediate

FINISHED SIZE

Basic edging: About
1/4 inch wide

Picot edging: About 1 inch
wide

MATERIALS

- 1 ball of turquoise crochet cotton cord in size 3

- Size B (2.25mm) crochet hook

- Tapestry needle

- Shirt with looped edging

GAUGE IN SINGLE CROCHET (SC)

20 sts = 4"

STITCHES USED

Chain (ch)

Single crochet (sc)

Slip stitch (sl st)

INSTRUCTIONS

SINGLE-CROCHET EDGING

Attach the cotton cord to a loop on the neck edge at the back of the shirt, sc in ea lp around the shirt. Cut the cord to 8 inches and pull the tail through the last lp. Weave in the end.

PICOT EDGING

Attach the cotton cord to a loop on the neck edge at the back of the shirt.

Row 1: Sc in ea lp around the shirt, join to the first st with a sl st.

Row 2: [Ch 5, sl st in the 3rd ch from hk, ch 2, sk 3 sts, sc in the next st] repeat around.

Weave in the end.

YARN USED

1 ball of Coats & Clark Yarns' *J. P. Coats Royal Fashion Crochet Thread*, size 3, 100% mercerized cotton, 150yd/137m in Warm Teal #0065.

Bead Crochet Necklace & Bracelet

Bead crochet necklaces were popular in the 1920s when many crocheters made them as long ropes. They would wrap them once or twice around their necks or tie them into a large knot in the middle. Once you're comfortable making this project, you might want to try working with even smaller beads and thread. You may find that working the first several rounds is the most difficult. But keep going. This jewelry is really worth making!

SKILL LEVEL

Advanced Intermediate

FINISHED SIZE

Necklace: 19 inches long

Bracelet: 7 1/2 to 8 inches

MATERIALS

- 1 ball of turquoise crochet cotton cord

- Size B (2.25mm) hook

- About 125 beads in each of five colors for necklace

- About 60 beads in each of three colors for bracelet

- Two cones each for the ends of the bracelet and necklace

- An accent bead for the bracelet

- A clasp for the necklace

- A large decorative bead or charm for the necklace

- Beading needle and thread to match beads

- Tapestry needle

GAUGE

Bracelet: 10 rows = 1"

Necklace: 6 rows = 1"

STITCHES USED

Chain (ch)

Single crochet (sc)

Slip stitch (sl st)

INSTRUCTIONS

BRACELET

Preparation

Tie a 10-inch length of thread to the crochet cotton and thread the beading needle. This allows you to string the beads onto the cotton using the thin

needle. String the beads onto the cord, stringing one of each color, and then repeat the pattern until all the beads are strung. Slide the knotted thread off the cord.

Foundation: Ch 3, do not turn.

Round 1: Sl st into the back half of the first ch, creating a circle, sl st into the back half of the next 2 ch.

Round 2: Sl st into the back half of ea st around.

Round 3: [Slide the hk into the back half of the next st, slide a bead down to the hk, yo, pull through the st and the lp on the hk] repeat around.

Round 4: [Slide the hk into the lp the bead is on in the next st, push the bead behind the hk, slide a bead down to the hk, yo, pull through the st and the lp on the hk] repeat around.

Repeat round 4 until the bracelet is the length you want, less the accent bead and two cones. Work two more rounds without beads. Weave in the ends.

ASSEMBLY

Attach beading thread to one of the ends of the bracelet and string a cone, an accent bead, and another cone, then secure the beads to the other end of the crochet cord and weave in the ends.

NECKLACE

Preparation

Tie a 10-inch length of thread to the crochet cotton, and thread the beading needle. This allows you to string the beads onto the cotton using the thin needle. String the beads onto the cord, stringing one of each color, and then repeat the pattern until all the beads are strung. Slide the knotted thread off the cord.

Foundation: Ch 5, do not turn.

Round 1: Sl st into the back half of the first ch, creating a circle, sl st into the back half of the next 4 ch.

Round 2: Sl st into the back half of ea st around.

Round 3: [Slide the hk into the back half of the next st, slide a bead down to the hk, yo, pull through the st and the lp on the hk] repeat around.

Round 4: [Slide the hk into the lp the bead is on in the next st, push the bead behind the hk, slide a bead down to the hk, yo, pull through the st and the lp on the hk] repeat around.

Repeat round 4 until the necklace is the length you want, less the two cones and the clasp. Work two more rounds without beads. Weave in the ends.

Attach beading thread to one of the ends of the necklace and string a cone, one of the beads from the necklace, and one end of the clasp.

Pass back through the bead and cone, and weave the thread end into the crochet cord. Repeat for the other side of the necklace with the other part of the clasp.

THE CHARM

String the charm on some beading thread, then string the beads. Make sure you string enough beads that will make a loop that is large enough to slide onto the necklace. Make your loop and tie the ends of the beading thread securely together. Slide the loop of beads onto your bead crochet necklace.

YARN USED

1 ball of Coats & Clark Yarn's *J. P. Coats Royal Fashion Crochet Thread*, size 3, 100% mercerized cotton, 150yd/137m, in Warm Teal #0065.

Just Charming

The decorative charm on the necklace came from an earring bought at a gift shop. You could make friendship necklaces by using a pair of earrings as charms for two neck-laces—then keep one for yourself and give the other to your special friend.

Acknowledgments

I wish to express my thanks to Joe Rhatigan for your deadlines and your help in modeling this book. And thank you so much, Jane LaFerla, for such a wonderful job of pulling this book together through the final stages. It's been a pleasure working with you. Thank you to the Dana Irwin, art director, for the cool layout, making this a fun and useful book; to Sandy Stambaugh for the fantastic photography that brings the projects alive; and to August Hoerr for his beautiful illustrations.

Many thanks especially to all the models—**Pearl Coogler, Leah Donatelli, Leah Haile, Christopher Hewitt, Natalie Hewitt, Zoe Jackson, Shirah Lee, Abby Lenderman, Skye Luke, Buna Selz-Mandell, Michael Probst, Faye Stevens**, and **Alex Villarreal**—for your happy faces that grace these pages.

Thank you to Katherine Blythe and Doris Erb at Patons for your help. And thank you to the following companies for supplying yarn for projects in this book:

Brown Sheep
Dale of Norway
Lorna's Laces
Plymouth Yarn Company
Patons
Reynolds Yarn
Tahki Imports Ltd.

Metric Conversion Table	
Inches	**Centimeters**
1/8	3 mm
1/4	6 mm
3/8	9 mm
1/2	1.3
5/8	1.6
3/4	1.9
7/8	2.2
1	2.5
1 1/4	3.1
1 1/2	3.8
1 3/4	4.4
2	5
2 1/2	6.25
3	7.5
3 1/2	8.8
4	10
4 1/2	11.3
5	12.5
5 1/2	13.8
6	15
7	17.5
8	20
9	22.5
10	25
11	27.5
12	30

Index